THE POWER OF

MASTERING THE 7 DYNAMIC LEARNING ZONES

LILI-ANN KRIEGLER

Praise for *The Power of Play*

The author's practical approach, drawn from multiple life experiences and a gift for language, makes this book a heartfelt and useful guide for educators. It is characterised by Gregory Bateson's (2000) sociological approach, offering the concept of being sensitive to everyday life patterns that connect into meaningful wholes. This book is not just another resource, but a unique perspective from an experienced educator, making it a valuable addition to any early childhood educator's library.

Dr Avis Ridgway, Monash University

In this book, Lili-Ann carefully takes the reader away from binary thinking, where free play opposes knowledge acquisition and asks us to reconsider our roles when working with young children. She invites educators to be active listeners and to see children's engagement and agency as paramount to learning. She reminds us that learning is as much about emotion as it is cognitive, and making connections and transferring knowledge should be our aim. Lili-Ann inspires educators to be intentional and aware of their practices and asks us to reconsider knowledge's role in early childhood education. She introduces us to her "7 learning zones", which are very helpful in analysing the role of the teacher and how our interactions with children mediate learning. It has been a joy to read and has given me another point of view to consider when working with students and teachers.

Shana Upiter, ELC Coordinator, Mount Scopus Memorial College

This is an enjoyable book with an approachable writing style that simplifies complex ideas. It's a strength of Lili-Ann's work, and I plan to recommend it to former colleagues and preschool teachers. Sadly, there's growing pressure on early educators to focus on academics at the expense of play-based, language-rich learning. Despite evidence that young children need experiences like these to build a foundation for later academic success, the belief persists that they should read by the age of four or five. I especially liked the section on language in Chapter 7. Lili-Ann provides valuable insights into how teachers can use language more effectively as a teaching tool. I hope this book brings her more opportunities to share her work.

Kelly Morgan, Canadian author and educator, Expert in Systematic Concept Teaching

Lili-Ann respects the Traditional Owners and Custodians of the land of the Kulin Nation groups, the Boonwurrung and Bunurong people, where she lives, learns and works.

Published in 2024 by Amba Press, Melbourne, Australia
www.ambapress.com.au

© Lili-Ann Kriegler 2024

All rights reserved. No part of this book may be reproduced or transmitted in any form or by any means, electronic or mechanical, including photocopying, recording or by any information storage and retrieval system, without prior permission in writing from the publisher.

Cover design: Tess McCabe
Internal design: Amba Press
Proofreader: Rica Dearman

ISBN: 9781923215382 (pbk)
ISBN: 9781923215399 (ebk)

A catalogue record for this book is available from the National Library of Australia.

Contents

Introduction		1
Part A: The vista		**3**
	Chapter 1 The confident educator	5
Part B: Concept foundation		**13**
	Chapter 2 Two tiers: Conceptualisation and cognition	17
	Chapter 3 Vertical knowledge	44
	Chapter 4 Distributed knowledge	55
	Chapter 5 Concept transfer	67
	Chapter 6 Avert the assessment avalanche	77
	Chapter 7 In words we meet the world	84
Part C: The agility wheel		**95**
	Chapter 8 The agility wheel	97
	Chapter 9 Free play	103
	Chapter 10 Mediated play	110
	Chapter 11 Embedded concepts	122
	Chapter 12 Clarity of concept	134
	Chapter 13 Closed-ended mobilisation	143
	Chapter 14 Open-ended mobilisation	150
	Chapter 15 Auto-generative creativity	158
	Chapter 16 The agile educator	167
Appendix: Lists for educators		**177**
Bibliography		191
Dedication		194
About the author		195

Introduction

Everything is easier if you start with confidence, and feeling competent is the bedrock of confidence. My wish for this book is that it amplifies your already established competence and, in turn, bolsters your students' sense of their competence.

There is little that intrigues and excites me more in my teaching role than seeing children in flow as they challenge themselves to learn, think, create and communicate. Concepts, insights, thoughts and the mastery of techniques and skills inspire and interest me whether they are encountered in preschool, primary, secondary or tertiary settings. This is equally true in my consultancy when educators encounter ideas and gain insights that transform their practice.

This book is a synthesis of what I have learned on my journey to understand knowledge at both the atomic level of language and concept acquisition and at the point where it is mobilised as a profound and marvellous vehicle for problem-solving and creativity.

I invite you to do two things. The first is to navigate a structured way of building children's concept formation from a pre-lingual status to an extraordinarily complex use of language.

The second is to explore seven distinctive learning zones that you can apply to assist your curriculum design or teaching. Each zone shows a relational configuration between educators and students. Within each zone, the proximity of the educator to the student changes. In some zones, the child has a wide range of choices and freedom. In others, the choices are limited to focus on specific learning goals. The book is a conversation about the agency of the student and the educator as they purposefully enact their intentions in what I think is the most critical endeavour in the world – education.

Throughout my childhood, my parents repeated the mantra: 'No one can take away your education; it will make you who you want to be'. I have become an educator, and I believe that the quality of education is curcial to creating a quality society.

I offer you my educational perspective based on what I have learned and experienced over more decades than I care to relay here! You will recognise the muses, sages, academics, theorists and philosophies that have influenced me. I am so grateful to have learned from others and from the long tradition of education that has led us to this moment.

This book is about educators' ability to adapt their skills, toolkits, knowledge and perspectives to optimise, understand, plan and assess different students and different elements in their context.

The book is designed in three parts:

- **Part A: The vista** – Reviewing the early education landscape
- **Part B: Concept foundation** – How concepts are constructed and used
- **Part C: The agility wheel** – Seven dynamic play and learning zones

There is also a comprehensive appendix of educator lists and resources to help you in the classroom.

I wrote this book for leaders, educators and curriculum coordinators in preschool and early primary settings. Although the ideas have broader applications, I dedicate this book to you and hope that in its pages, you will come across ideas and information that will inform your practice and add to your knowledge about knowledge.

PART A

THE VISTA

REVIEWING THE EARLY EDUCATION LANDSCAPE

Chapter 1
The confident educator

If we know better, we can do better.
Maya Angelou

Would you like to enhance and energise your early years' teaching? The key to positive transformation is trusting your professional knowledge. Knowledge gives you confidence and clarity when you plan, assess, resource, enact and data-track your practice. Your enhanced teaching translates into children's elevated thinking and learning.

This book is for early years educators; to clarify the terminology, 'early years' includes preschool and junior primary education designed for children aged three to nine years, while 'educator' is an umbrella term for all the early years professionals working with young children, including preschool assistants, teacher aides, degree-qualified teachers, leaders and curriculum coordinators, all of whom play a vital role.

A key goal of this book is to add value to your practice without adding time to your schedule. The intention is that it will offer you a concept-based lens to review what you already do well.

The 'why' of an early childhood educator

More and more research indicates that early education is critically important. By the age of five, 90% of the brain's neural networks are laid down (Schonkoff & Phillips, 2000), and the number of words and quality of language a child has been exposed to has already started to determine how well they will succeed in later life (Suskind, 2015).

These are great reasons to be inspired to do your best job!

Knowing your practice allows you to develop laser-sharp planning and highly efficient assessment and reporting. It also assures you that your school or centre is accountable in the face of compliance demands from any education authority.

Sadly, rather than feeling positive, many early childhood educators experience a sense of being overwhelmed by expectations – which seem to be coming at them from every direction. More than in any other education phase, there are confusing messages, conflicting philosophies, constant debates and strong opinions in the early years arena. Educators sometimes don't even know if what they are requested to do is compulsory or just someone's preferred approach. Teachers end up with decision paralysis and don't know where to turn because of conflicting expectations and criticism.

What is the source of uncertainty and confusion in the early years?

It is commonly believed, and there is ample research to prove it (Singer et al., 2006), that children learn through play. However, the minute we use the word 'play', we polarise the early learning community. Some early primary teachers automatically switch off when they hear the word 'play' because their students are not in preschool, which they see as the appropriate context for play. In their minds, they have a set learning curriculum, and 'play' does not come into it. Parents have a powerful influence on ideas about play at the primary level, often characterising it as a waste of time; some parents don't want to hear that their children are 'only playing'.

On the other hand, some early childhood teachers feel as though they cannot directly 'teach' because they are told so often that children learn through play. They develop a hands-off approach and leave the children to it. Yet, as you have just read above, the early years are a critical time for learning.

Children do learn through play, but they don't *only* learn through play.

We must ask ourselves, 'What is at the heart of this debate?' and the answer is something more profound.

The debate is about agency

Children's agency is about having autonomy and independence.

There is an opinion that preschool teachers engage in direct teaching to the detriment of the young child's independence or creativity. Children ought to be left alone to discover knowledge rather than have it taught to them directly. A typical quote states that 'play is a child's work'. There is a fear that if content is taught in the kindergarten room, the child is being subjected to a push-down curriculum.

Conversely, young children are expected to become strong, involved learners. If they leave kindergarten and are not 'school ready', then the early years teacher has not achieved their goals for that child. The result of this paradox is paralysis of action. What do we do?

Many fear that learning too much too early leads to stress and a lack of motivation. There is no doubt this can happen. If students are challenged beyond what the renowned educational psychologist Lev Vygotsky called their 'zone of proximal development', stress could build in the learning relationship (Vygotsky, 1978, p. 81; McLeod, 2019). This includes frustration, resentment, stubbornness, blocking and many more emotional outcomes. Although we frame learning as a mental act, it is also both emotional and cognitive (Feuerstein et al., 2009).

The rationale for a book on conceptual understanding in the current educational climate

This distinction has become even more relevant in the post-COVID era. Research shows that many children's social and emotional development did not advance as usual during the lockdowns. With less social experience and fewer skills, they appear to struggle more than expected to fit into groups and to learn and navigate daily challenges. Educators report an increase in social and emotional issues.

Of course, this is no easy situation. But if we concentrate solely on the emotional aspect of this circumstance, we use only half of our arsenal to improve it. As research by the cognitive psychologist Reuven Feuerstein reports, emotion and cognition are two sides of the same coin.

At the most simplistic level, emotion might relate to whether a child is happy about completing a task. However, when we talk about learning emotion, it is more about the energy a child brings to the situation. It is about children's motivation to learn.

Dr Ferre Laevers' simple tool for determining if a child is doing OK uses a five-point scale to further validate the necessity of both cognition and emotion in sound learning. The **Leuven Scale**, developed at Leuven University in Belgium, assesses the **emotional wellbeing** and **involvement** of children in educational settings (MacRae & Jones, 2019). It includes five levels for emotional wellbeing, ranging from **extremely low** (signs of discomfort) to **extremely high** (happy, cheerful, self-confident). Involvement levels measure whether children operate at their full capabilities during activities, from **low activity** (simple, repetitive) to **high involvement** (focused, engaged). High wellbeing and involvement contribute to emotional intelligence and mental health, leading to better child development and deep-level learning. When you unpack this, it is a relationship between feeling positive and active engagement. There is a mutual relationship between them. Therefore, one of the ways to ensure emotional wellbeing is to keep the children active.

Why is this book timely?

Both Laevers' and Feuerstein's research shows that one of the most powerful ways to alter a child's emotional state is through cognition. The way to improve wellbeing is to think about it. This means clearly understanding emotions by naming them as they are being felt. Furthermore, emotional wellbeing improves when children learn coping strategies to counteract negative feelings.

As Vygotsky has alerted us, there is a delicate art to maintaining motivation and providing the challenge that is within reach but not too easy. The zone has a floor and a ceiling – you don't want to move beyond either. So, agency relates to motivation as well as to autonomy. In this book, we ask:

> *How can play, thinking and learning cohere in early education to achieve the outcome that both the students and the educators have an equal role; that the agency of both is honoured?*

Learning loses its lustre without motivational energy, a sense of purpose, autonomy and a degree of choice.

Structure does not reduce creativity

There is a fear among educators that if we structure knowledge too tightly, we interfere with children's creativity. However, unless the tasks are prescriptive, this is not the case.

An organised, structured introduction to knowledge puts a child in a position to be even more creative because they have more information to fuel their creative outputs. We and they can imagine more complex play because as knowledge increases, the quality of play spirals to a new and more sophisticated level. And the quality of what they produce is informed by more sophisticated skills.

Collaborative learning

Further to the above debates, some want to see young children learning collaboratively in groups and not as individuals. There is a strong push to develop collaborative projects. The issue is assessing and tracking an individual child's progress within the group.

How do we resolve these conflicting concerns?

In the face of conflicting ideas, educators feel pressured to choose a position. If they accept that children learn through play, they might retreat from planning a structured curriculum and direct teaching. It is possible that with too much freedom, the child's knowledge won't be elevated during play. If they want to ensure that children learn the concepts needed for them to be school-ready, educators might structure the children's content tasks too prescriptively and allow too little freedom. To ensure every child has 'got it', the products are identical.

Children who do not play miss the essential social experience, freedom and intentional activity. If not taught, they miss the opportunity to develop their knowledge and understanding, forming the foundation for thinking and learning throughout their lives.

None of the elements discussed above arrived out of thin air. There are good reasons for children to play, sound reasons for them to receive tuition and a long history of structured curricula for children of all ages. There is also great benefit in both individual and collaborative learning.

Trans-heritance rather than transmission

So, why not use *all of these learning configurations* to our advantage? The debates and divisions don't serve early childhood educators. Rather than saying that direct teaching affects a child's freedom, we can reframe this. If we avoid sharing knowledge, early years education becomes an island isolated from the education mainland. Rather than thinking of knowledge as forcible sharing or transmission, I envision learning in the early years as a trans-heritance of knowledge.

Young children are equally entitled to the knowledge of humanity. They are thinkers, they are wise and they want to know things. Their learning cannot be disconnected from world knowledge. If we offer opportunities to learn in appealing ways so that children can engage richly with it, their immersion in it will generate their unique perspectives. They will teach us things that augment our own knowledge. Like older students, they deserve a serious encounter with knowledge and expertise.

Moving away from binary thinking

As educators, we will benefit from moving away from binary, either-or thinking and settling all these positions on a continuum. Once we understand the elements on the continuum, we can move between them and use the appropriate ones for specific goals or to respond to unique daily situations. If we don't maximise knowledge and perspectives, each day's opportunities for learning and quality play might be lost.

In my work as an education consultant and seminar presenter for the past 12 years and before that as a director of early learning, I have realised that there is a need to come to grips with the debates and develop a means to transform early childhood educators into confident, agile operators. We need to become agile to adapt our knowledge and skills to any learning situation. I think of educators as chameleons, remarkable creatures that can adapt their colours for any situation and environment. Let us be agile enough to use all our knowledge and skills as we work with young children.

I have represented the continuum in this book with an agility wheel.

The agility wheel allows us to move between different learning zones and apply the requisite skills to any situation.

Seven learning zones

From my leadership and teaching practice, I've identified seven characteristic learning zones that operate in classrooms. Within each zone I noticed how the educator and student interaction changed. Once educators understand the features of each zone, they can move between them with a purpose. Understanding the zones supported me with planning, assessment, resourcing and reporting. My ongoing thinking and the experience of listening to scores of educators during my consultancy and reading established research have given me even greater clarity about these learning configurations. This clarity is what I want to share with you in this book.

The zones are:

1. Free play
2. Mediated play
3. Embedded concepts
4. Concept clarity
5. Closed-ended mobilisation
6. Open-ended mobilisation
7. Auto-generative creativity

Across this continuum, the educator adapts their proximity, moving closer when needed and moving away when not. Each zone has specific goals and interactions. It is essential right from the start to see that these zones are not stages. Instead, they are ways of interacting with children and mediating their learning. The child could be in the middle of free exploration, and the educator might decide to step in for three seconds to directly teach the name of some object or process, then immediately step away again. Skilful adaptability allows teachers to maximise their practices and artfully arrange learning environments.

The learning zones are presented in detail in Part C of the book.

A focus on concepts

Before we get there, you will have noticed that a couple of learning zones include the word 'concept'. Concepts are how we package knowledge. The next three chapters are devoted to expanding on the knowledge that supports these learning zones.

Core questions to consider

From what you have read in this chapter, how would you guide your practice? Are you currently more focused on the playing or learning side of the scale? Are your beliefs reflected in your school or centre's philosophy, vision and curriculum? Did anything surprise you? Are you ready to learn more about knowledge and the learning zones with each of its specific toolkits?

Let's get going to the next section.

PART B

CONCEPT FOUNDATION

HOW CONCEPTS ARE CONSTRUCTED AND USED

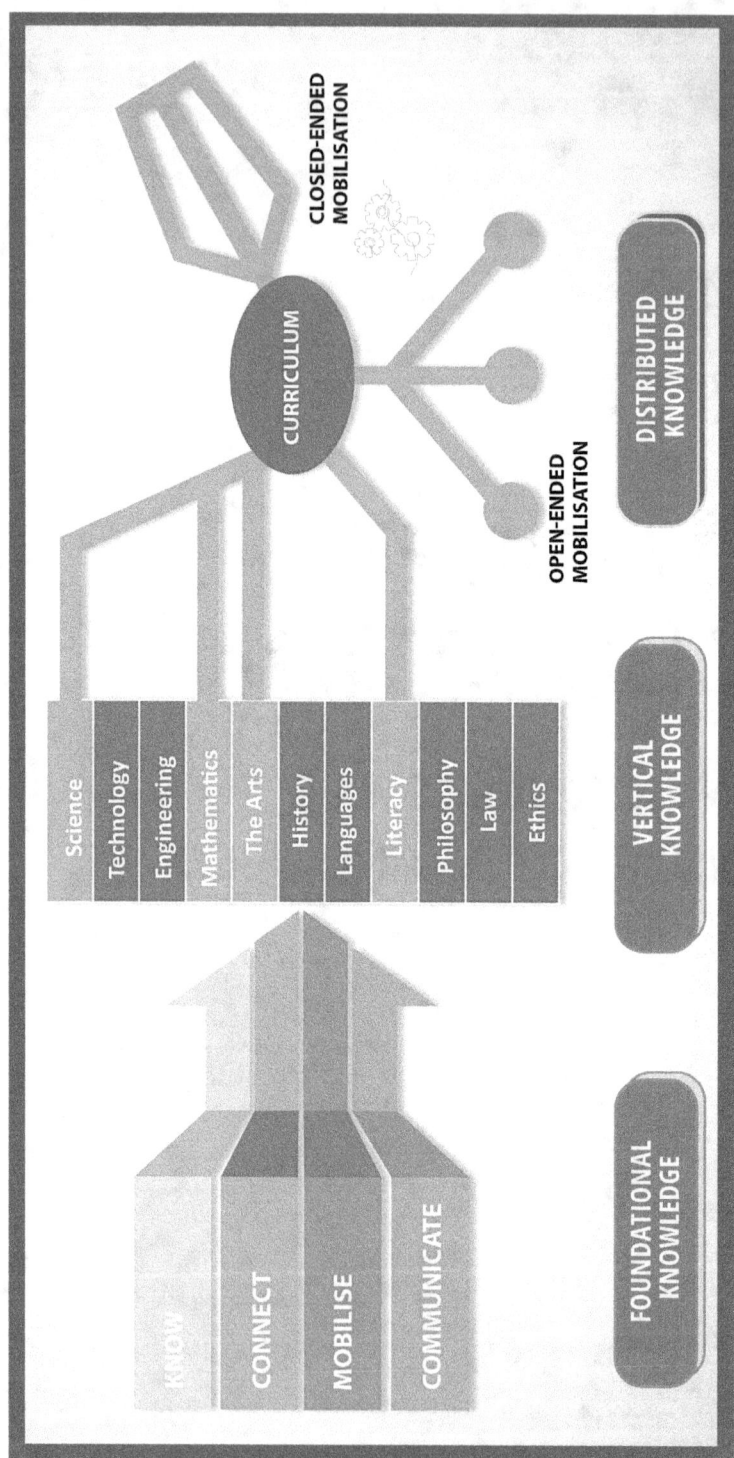

Figure 1: Three knowledge categories

This book discusses children's concept-based understanding and how it is supported and scaffolded within Part C's seven distinctive learning zones on an agility wheel.

I want to familiarise you with how concepts are formed and activated in the learning curriculum to help you follow how the concepts are being constructed and utilised within the zones.

To do this, I have created a graphic diagram displaying three knowledge categories you will continue to encounter as you read. The categories are:

1. **Foundational knowledge.** All learning is based on foundational knowledge. I will soon introduce you to four terms to explain this: know, connect, mobilise and communicate. Foundational knowledge is represented in the graphic as the basis of all other learning.

2. **Vertical knowledge.** Vertical knowledge is a term borrowed from Edward de Bono, who called all existing knowledge vertical knowledge. You will see it as a standard classification of disciplines from which we derive our curricula. Examples are science or the arts, etc. Engagement with subject areas is fuelled by foundational concept formation (De Bono, 1998).

3. **Distributed knowledge.** Distributed knowledge is a term I have created to represent the unique and infinite ways we collaborate in immersive learning. It refers to how new knowledge is made when it is distributed by the actors involved in projects and learning tasks. Distributed knowledge draws on vertical knowledge but is customised by us. We and our students repackage and redraw knowledge and skills to achieve unique curriculum goals.

   Distributed knowledge is alive and dynamic, populated by knowledge actors, including educators, students, families and communities. This form of knowledge is a creative endeavour free from existing limitations. It is democratic, fully mobilised and constantly evolving. Its vibrancy stems from being grounded in the present and actively contributing to the creation of the future.

Throughout the book, you will find the motifs of closed-ended and open-ended mobilisation. Sometimes, we operate in the known, the predictable, the tried and the tested, but often, we are researching, innovating, projecting and creating. Conceptual understanding is vital for both closed-ended and open-ended systems.

In Part B, concept foundation, I will present chapters covering information about:

- The distinction between conceptual understanding and cognition
- Four different kinds of foundational knowledge
- The origin of curriculum content from vertical subject areas
- An exploration of distributed knowledge related to:
    - curriculum planning
    - transfer of knowledge
    - assessment
    - language structure
    - ways to support language and conceptual understanding

Once you have read these chapters, you will quickly see how concepts are used and scaffolded for children in the seven learning zones in Part C.

Chapter 2
Two tiers: Conceptualisation and cognition

Study the science of art. Study the art of science. Develop your senses – especially learn how to see. Realise that everything connects to everything else.

Leonardo da Vinci

Whether you work in the early years or any other phase of education, your currency is knowledge. Broadly, knowledge is divided into *content* and *process*.

Content is the 'what', and process is the 'how'.

Content is conceptual learning – and the process is cognition.

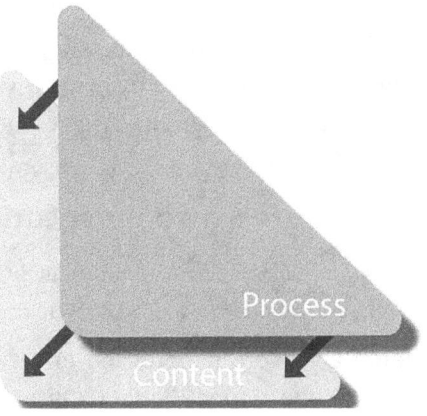

Figure 2: Two-tiered learning

What is a concept?

Looking around us, we can see hundreds of things in our immediate environment. A table, a chair, a wall, a flower arrangement, a packet of biscuits, a cat.

We use labels to name each of these recognised objects without thinking about them. The label represents an object or idea. By applying a label, we enter conceptual and abstract thinking. We can 'think' about the cat when we leave the room. We can even think about our specific cat in relation to other cats. We know that cats are pets, and that by being pets they are like dogs, goldfish and, in my daughter's case, a six-foot python!

What is process?

In the short discussion about concepts above, besides *labelling*, other processes emerged. *Knowing, representing, thinking, comparing, categorising, recollecting, connecting, remembering.* These are all *processes* for managing knowledge. They are thinking actions.

When we are alerted to our thinking processes, and consciously use them, we think at another level. Understanding our thinking is metacognition. I recently attended an online course with a British early childhood specialist, Dr Ruth Deutsch, to study the Bright Start Program developed by a recently deceased cognitive researcher from Vanderbilt professor, Carl Haywood (Haywood, 2003). She said *'You can't start to develop metacognition too early!'* And there is research to back the benefit of explicitly teaching metacognition (Ellis et al., 2013; Ronilo, 2018).

When I say explicitly teaching, I don't mean teaching the skills in isolation. I believe in including reference to them in context while teachers and students are approaching, acquiring and merging content.

Concepts are separated into two categories

Lower-order concepts are labels for the objects and ideas as single specific instances in the real world. For example, I have a ruler on my desk.

Higher-order concepts are more generalised and refer to a group of lower-order concepts that share identifiable features/criteria that make them eligible to be included in a category. A ruler is part of a category called 'instruments of measurement' and shares the category with a thermometer, a barometer, a metronome and a bathroom scale. Besides cataloguing objects into categories, we can categorise features of an object. Big, small, medium, minuscule, expansive and tiny are all features of 'size'.

Higher-order concepts are efficient because they are transferable across contexts. If I know that size as a concept, I can use it in maths, geography, literacy, dressmaking, carpentry, surgery and many other contexts. Packaging information in high-order concepts is one of the ways we can teach for transfer.

The advantage of general categories is that they help us to organise our knowledge.

We use processes to develop categories. Developing both content and process knowledge simultaneously can be called two-tier teaching. In two-tier teaching, we consciously surface and direct students' attention to their thinking skills as we navigate content with them.

Content knowledge, from the simplest to the most complex, is *conceptual*. How we manage, use, organise and deploy process knowledge is *cognition*.

Once, when I was discussing how we think with four-year-olds, a child called Daniel described how, in his brain, he had a huge cupboard with hundreds of tiny drawers. He put an idea in a drawer and remembered where it was. When he wanted it again, he just opened the drawer and took it out.

His metaphor is quite helpful.

What is in the drawers is the *content*.

The cupboard and the drawers are the organisational structure.

The *processes* involve knowing where the drawers are, opening them, retrieving the knowledge and using it.

There are two things to say about this metaphor. First, we don't want the structure of our knowledge to be set in stone (or wood). So, systems thinking is a better metaphor from our perspective. If one thing changes in a system, everything adjusts. In systems thinking, we don't end up with old information in the drawers that is no longer relevant, true or appropriate. The system updates to reflect new information.

Jean Piaget's terms of assimilation and accommodation are good for explaining this. Assimilation is how you understand it at first, and accommodation is how it changes in the light of new information (Piaget & Cook, 1952).

The second thing to say about conceptual information and cognition is that the distinction can become confusing, and for good reason. If I talk about comparison, I am labelling a mental activity. Therefore, it is a concept. But if I am engaged in the act of comparing, if I am in the flow of it, then it is a process. Cognition is the act of using the thinking process.

I can put 'comparison' in one of Daniel's drawers. I can even put a variety of systems for comparison in the drawer. While I'm comparing all the drawers and selecting which drawer to put them into, I'm mobilising cognition. Cognition happens in the present. It is a current state. If I say now that I was comparing things yesterday, it is a memory and a piece of content. As I write this, I am trying to organise the concepts in a particular order so that they are understandable to you. When I read this back, it is already content.

There are labels and definitions for things – content, and the active minute-by-minute use of processes – cognition.

Knowing your knowledge

Several years ago, I designed an educational leadership seminar series attended by preschool and lower primary leaders, curriculum coordinators and educators. Over several encounters, they were challenged to define their educational philosophy and curriculum vision. Despite knowledge being central to their work, uncertainty about knowledge arose as their number one concern! It was a surprise to all of us. And it wasn't merely a lack of clarity about planning an appropriate curriculum. There were questions about assessment, reporting, compliance, communication with parents and forging relationships with specialists. What we realised was that they couldn't fully distinguish between the different kinds of knowledge they were offering. They hadn't consciously and purposefully defined, evaluated or curated it in their minds, so it was not being done on paper.

The first distinction was the one above, which states that knowledge is conceptual and cognitive. But there are more refined ways of looking at knowledge. After grappling with knowledge for years, I had abbreviated it in my mind to four words: know, connect, mobilise and communicate.

Know, connect, mobilise, communicate

After expanding on these four entry points, the participants were on firmer ground in matching their curriculum planning to reflect their educational ideals. They were also clearer about how to arrange and resource their play and learning environments. With a high-level vision in place and more certainty about content, they worked out ways to evaluate students' learning that dovetailed with their values and vision. They became much more confident about enacting their leadership roles.

A valuable insight they gained during this seminar series was that what you see is often limited by what you're looking for. If you know more or expect more, you find more. Their planning and especially their evaluation became more targeted to match their goals.

Acquiring and consolidating concepts is easy for some children and occurs as if by osmosis. But mostly there is no consistent, automatic maturational path. It helps considerably if children are alerted to concepts, become conscious of them and consolidate them with the immediate contexts where they occur (Kinard & Kozulin, 2008).

Four components of foundational knowledge

1. Know
2. Connect
3. Mobilise
4. Communicate

I want to share these four knowledge entry points with you in more detail so that, like the educators referred to above, you can distinguish, evaluate and curate them. You might decide how they align with your own vision or the philosophical ideals of your context. You can determine if and how they operate in your day-to-day work, and perhaps be inspired to incorporate them more consciously into your own planning and evaluation. As we go along, you will see that the thinking processes are discussed alongside the content. At the end of each section you will find a list of process words.

Take a deep breath!

Figure 3: Pictorial representation of four kinds of knowledge

1. Know

Perception

Before we can use knowledge in any way, we need to be aware of it. From birth, children are constantly learning to recognise things and assign meaning to them.

There is an order.

First, a child receives information through their sensory pathways, then, through repeated exposure, they recognise a pattern. The pattern can be a series of events which become predictable, or the recognition of an entity.

(Of course, they don't use the word 'entity'! They just know that it tastes good and it comes regularly – like milk!)

An infant hears footsteps; next, they are raised up and hugged warmly by a parent, grandparent or some lovely entity. They recognise the bottle and know it contains the drink they like and need. Over time, they give meaning to these sensory experiences, patterns and entities. Much later, they learn to name and label them. Sensing, without assigning meaning, is just sensing. Assigning meaning to an experience is perception. So, the first step in *knowing* something is perception (Yasnitsky et al., 2014, p. 70).

Children know things before they can label them. They build up experiential schemas (a bit like a sensory memory) in their mind that they may not have a word for (Hill, 2016; Atherton & Nutbrown, 2013). This kind of knowledge gathers information from immediate experience and personal points of view – and that is exactly what young children do when they play and why play is so important.

Sensory experiences become motor-perceptual memories.

Later in life, say, in a science laboratory, the knowledge of how liquid moves in a bucket, learnt as a child, enables a researcher not to spill sulphuric acid from a beaker onto a bench. Students build up multisensory memories in their minds, and they learn how the world works.

An example of sensory understanding occurred during a storytelling drama incursion organised when I was still teaching. The performer was dressed as a fairy called Little Sky Blue. During the performance, a storm damaged her wing and the children were invited to 'fix it' for her.

Clearly, she was not fairy-sized! After her performance, we asked the children if she was 'real'. We were not surprised that they said emphatically, 'NO!' It was surprising that it had nothing to do with her size, which they could easily have articulated. It was the quality of her wings.

They couldn't tell us that real fairies' wings are translucent, insubstantial, fragile or ethereal... because they didn't have the vocabulary. But they did have the concept. They tried to tell us by using their hands, demonstrating these ideas with soft, fluttery movements and gestures.

Learning is not based on facts. It is a fact when you have a name for it, and you can share and articulate it. But you can know it long before then. This is important to remember in the early years because 'qualities' or 'feelings' of things are what children internalise when they play with and manipulate a vast array of materials every day. A child learns about balancing water in a bucket by experiencing balancing water in a bucket many times.

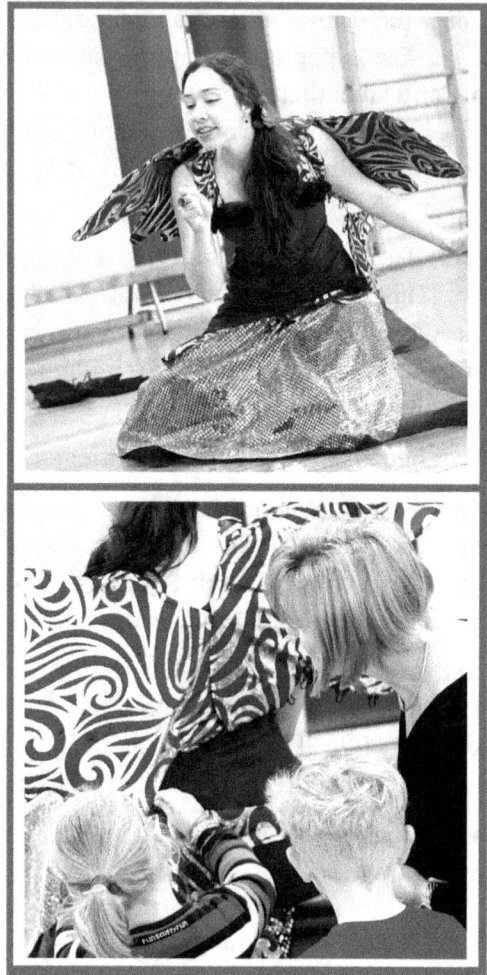

Figure 4: Fairy incursion – fixing broken wing

Attaching labels

Beyond experiential schemas, where children know things without naming them, we get to where they learn labels for them. There may be a stage when they give their own partial names for things. Grandpa is 'Da'.

People in their circle will understand these. It is idiosyncratic language. Some identical twins develop an entire idiosyncratic language only they understand.

It makes me think of the entertaining scene in the Disney version of *The Little Mermaid* (1989) where the seagull, Scuttle, knowledgeably informs the mermaid, Ariel, that a fork is a *dinglehopper*.

'Humans use these little babies to straighten their hair out! Just a little twirl here, and you got an aesthetically pleasing configuration of hair that humans go nuts over!'

How was Ariel to know any different?

Knowing the facts and what something is is essential, but it is static. Very often, in early years and other educational settings, an educator asks for nothing more than recognition.

'What shape is this?'

'A square.'

'Great answer.'

Visualisation

A stage beyond recognising and naming an entity is the ability to hold a mental image of it in your mind. This visualisation or mental imagery is vital because it enables us to think about things that are not immediately perceptible. Children recognise a chair before them but must also learn to picture it when it is not there. Some people, believe it or not, do not have this ability – this is called *aphantasia*. When I first heard this, I was agog because holding pictures in my mind is second nature. Right now, I see and smell a virtual coffee!

Mental images are the immediate way we begin to represent the real world in our minds. They move us from the concrete here and now into the abstract world. Children learn to name and picture things in their minds.

But we want children to do more than know what something is. We want them to connect their knowledge to everything else. I love how Da Vinci expresses this idea in the quote at the start of this chapter: quite simply, 'Everything connects to everything else.'

Thinking is habitual. We get used to doing it in a particular way. If we want children aged three to nine years to spontaneously try to connect the dots between different pieces of information, we must encourage them to do it regularly so that they lay down a neural pathway to do it. We want connecting to become habitual. We want them to have neural superhighway for connecting stuff.

> ***Process words:*** *sensing, experiencing, focusing, perceiving, recognising, assigning meaning, remembering, labelling*

In summary

- Infants start learning things from birth (and possibly before)
- Information enters through the sensory pathways
- The brain responds to, and begins to interpret, patterns in entities and events
- When the pattern or sensation is assigned meaning, it is perception
- Children may have experiential schemas in their minds before they can name and label what they know
- In a social or educational setting, the pieces of knowledge are given names and labels
- Initially, the labels may be idiosyncratic and understood only by people close to the child
- Conventional names and labels are ascribed to both concrete and abstract entities
- The same or similar entities are recognised in diverse contexts
- The entity is available as a mental image which represents the real thing in the real world

2. Connect

There are many ways to connect knowledge. Perhaps the most logical place to start is to connect something to itself. Internal connections.

Whole and parts

Beyond recognition, knowledge becomes more complex; and we don't have to go too far to explore this complexity. We can start by simply unpacking the whole and parts of a single entity. (I know! I love the word 'entity'. 'Object' does not do it for me. I can't think of a tree or a dog as an object.)

An entity is something with an individual and specific existence. Let's again use the square mentioned earlier, when the educator was asking what this shape was. If we extend thinking past recognition, we can unpack the features of a square. Four equal straight sides, four 90° corners. (And there are MANY more features of a square.) If our entity is a mandarin, then the features are that it has an inside and an outside. The outside is peel, the inside is segments. It has juice in it.

As you can see, the minute we start to unpack the whole and parts of a single thing, we are already connecting. We identify relationships between the whole and the parts. The mandarin segments have curved shapes and are triangular at the top. This is so that they nest together in the cylindrical shape of the fruit. If we go from the whole and unpack the parts we are *analysing*, if we go from the parts, see how they work together and pack them back, we are *synthesising*. Synthesis and analysis are also sometimes called inductive and deductive reasoning.

To challenge everything I just said, a whole is not always one integral thing. For example, a team consisting of 11 players is a whole.

Comparison

After analysing an individual entity in whole and parts, we compare one thing to another. It makes sense, at first, to compare what is the same or similar about the things we are focusing on and then, later, to explore what is different.

Initially, the square may be compared to a rectangle, and the mandarin may be compared to a lemon. They have several similarities. When we connect ideas, we understand the features of each individual thing; then we focus on the similarities and differences in those features in something else. The rectangle and the square are similar in all aspects except for one feature. The square has four sides of the same length, the rectangle has two sets of two equal sides.

The mandarin is first compared to a lemon and later to a banana, which, despite being a fruit, is very different according to several features: shape, structure, flavour, texture, etc.

Comparison is not a single thinking skill. It's a compact battery of individual skills.

We have ordered steps:
- Define a focus entity A and a target entity B
- Observe the focus and target entities in detail
- Plan a goal for the comparison
- Determine the criteria for comparison
- Discard what is irrelevant
- Come to a conclusion about the comparison process (Feuerstein et al., 1980)

A comparison makes thinking more efficient.

What can the comparison relate to?

Comparison shows how things are equivalent, similar or different by size, distance, volume, height, form, position, weight, orientation, function, age, effort, complexity, beauty, value, temperature... and capacity to annoy you. These are all criteria and each gives us a specific kind of information. There are endless ways of connecting information through comparison, and it can give us clarity about one thing in the light of another.

Children can enhance their ability to compare at an early age. When comparing two of their friends, we can guide them to select specific criteria rather than do a hazy comparison. They compare height, hair colour, loyalty, personality and many other features. We call this ability comparing apples with apples. This targeted thinking and comparing is a very transferable skill.

A further fundamental aspect of comparison is to keep track of what remains the same and what has changed. For example, if six oranges have been cut into quarters, there are 24 pieces, but the fact remains that all the parts originate from six oranges. This is the conservation of constancy – tracking what is the same.

When we match similar things, we begin to sort them into groups.

Categorisation/classification

When things are similar, like the mandarin and the lemon, we can categorise them. In this case, they belong to the superordinate category: citrus fruits. A superordinate category is the next group up from the element we are dealing with. Mandarin is a citrus fruit; next up is fruit; and next up might be food type.

The square and the rectangle belong to the superordinate category: two-dimensional linear shapes, because they are composed of straight lines and enclose an area. Categorisation and classification are umbrella words for elements that belong together. Dedre Gentner, a foremost language researcher, has demonstrated that comparison processes are central in children's learning of relational knowledge in categories (Gentner, 2005).

You will no doubt see this bring order and organisation to our knowledge. It has been doing this since time immemorial. For instance, in biology, animals and plants have been classified into different species.

It is important to remember that depending on the focus feature, a single entity can belong to more than one category. For example, a red circle can belong to both colour and shape categories. This is the basis of Venn diagrams. A person may be a sibling and a spouse.

Categorisation has two parts: the superordinate category and the elements. Let's say that a child is out in the rain. Someone says, 'It's wet weather today' – that gives some information.

We could just park that.

But if we say, 'Do you remember the other day when it hailed? That was really stormy weather! What do you think hail is made of?'

A child might respond, 'It was made of ice, and I know ice is made of water. It made my hands freeze!'

Then we ask: 'And what is rain made of?'

'Water.'

'Yep, and is there any other weather where water is important?'

The child is building up a portfolio of knowledge about the weather. The superordinate concept starts to inform the elements, and the elements make the superordinate category more understandable, too. This is a two-way mechanism for consolidating meaning and information.

When they encounter snow, sleet, drizzle, mizzle, mist or fog, they might have a better understanding of the weather and each of these unique kinds of weather. Categories are a way of generalising knowledge, going from the specific and particular to the universal. The universal is good for transfer.

In his future-focused education, Lee Watanabe-Crockett describes a series of herding questions, which move progressively from the specific to the general. At the general level, everyone can think about an issue from exactly where they are (Watanabe-Crockett, 2018). If we apply this idea in the early years, we might get something like this:

- Is Robin a good friend?
- Is Robin a better friend than Jules?
- What is a good friend?
- What is friendship?

Or:

- Do you like the rain?
- Is rain better than wind?
- Which is your favourite kind of weather?
- What is weather?

So, the effort spent connecting the specific to the general is time well spent.

Identifying connection in children's speech

Here is a piece of documentation where friends Harry and Nicholas (both aged four) are considering the weather:

Harry: *'This time is when the weather changes. It changes to different times for the year.'*

Harry relates weather to the concept of time. This conversation could be extended if we ask him what happens at different times of the year. We could ask him to elaborate on his knowledge.

When Nicholas is asked to comment, he says:

'We're at the first sign of what he said. It's not the cold season yet, because the cold season is after the hot season, and it's next term or next year. It can change. It's like rain, or a storm or the deep snow... I haven't seen that here. But I saw it on the TV when Mole was inside, and the snow was on the outside, and sometimes it's dark, and sometimes it's light...'

Nicholas's response is almost like that of James Joyce's novel *Ulysses*, famous for its stream of consciousness! He moves through multiple concepts and contexts within this short explanation.

First, he acknowledges that he is responding to Harry's earlier contribution. He recognises the *convention* of picking up a thread and responding within a recognised discourse. Then, he thinks about the sequence of *time* in seasons, school terms and the light or dark of passing days. He distinguishes between *kinds* of weather. This indicates that he has not experienced extreme weather in this *place* in the same way he did in another place he remembers. We hear about his pastime of watching television in relation to his *literary* knowledge of Kenneth Grahame's character, Mole, from *Wind in the Willows*. He also uses some references to orientation in *space*, referring to 'here' as Australia, as opposed to England, his country of origin. He uses the spatial terms 'inside' and 'outside'. The interweaving of ideas is like a complex and beautiful thought melody.

We could continue the conversation with Nicholas to solidify or extend his understanding of the concepts he is exploring, but he is already excellent at connecting ideas.

Knowing and connecting as static knowledge

So far in this discussion, we see the connection of information, but we are still in an area of static knowledge. We have information about single entities and how they are the same or different from others. We can see the relationships between them. The knowledge is not yet mobilised.

But don't underestimate the immense value of this knowledge. If we don't know exactly what criteria, attributes or features things have and how they are the same or different from one another, the concepts won't be consolidated enough to mobilise them!

Some readers might be thinking, 'Surely this kind of matching and understanding relationships is mobilising knowledge?' If the thinking is used in evaluation and decision-making, it is mobilisation. If it is just noting the relationships, it is static.

For example, you go to purchase a car. There is a black car and a red car. You know the horsepower of each. Static knowledge.

You want to decide which to buy. The black car has more horsepower and will give more grunt. You primarily drive your car in an urban area with 50–100kmph speed limits. You are concerned about safety, and red is more visible. Your favourite colour for cars is black. Based on these considerations, which car would you choose? Mobilised knowledge.

Another way that comparison is mobilised is in figurative language. In literature or in life things are often compared abstractly, which shifts their meaning from their original location. 'His skin was yellowed parchment.' In this metaphorical language, parchment – old-fashioned writing material – is used to describe someone's skin. This uses inferential thinking. You are not told but have to work out what it means by to use features of parchment to describe skin.

> ***Process words:*** *focusing, attending, analysing, synthesising, comparing, relating, categorising, evaluating, decision-making, inferring*

In summary

- When we connect an object to itself, we gain understanding of the internal relationships between a whole and the features of its parts
- We compare using a small set of subskills
- We compare a focus entity A to a target entity B
- We select specific features or criteria to compare by
- We discard irrelevant information
- We look for the equivalence, similarity or difference of a specific feature between focus A and target B
- When teaching, it is generally more efficient to start comparisons by looking at what is the same or similar, and then moving on to what is different
- When we understand the criteria, similarities and differences, we are in a position to categorise or classify information
- Categorisation gives a deeper understanding of both the umbrella concept and the elements within it
- Connection helps to locate and organise knowledge for more accessible learning, retrieval, mobilisation and transfer

3. Mobilise

As we have seen, connected knowledge, even if static, is extremely important. But knowing and connecting knowledge is different from mobilising knowledge.

When we mobilise knowledge, we apply it to achieve a goal. I have already raised the idea that even making a decision mobilises knowledge. To make a decision, we evaluate something and project the consequences of a course of action.

How do children mobilise knowledge?

Young children usually know their colours: blue, red and yellow. They connect that shades of blue are similar in colour to the primary colour blue, that blue is different from yellow, and that all three are colours. Knowledge is mobilised when something is done with it.

Children might sort the colours into groups. This often happens when children are playing with blocks and other loose parts. They use all the blue wishing stones in one area, all the green in another and all the yellow somewhere else. They might have the blue stones represent water and the green ones represent grass.

Once they learn that you can create secondary colours by mixing the primary colours, they activate the knowledge at the painting easel as they try to get the exact colour orange to paint marigolds. They might even add white to lighten their colours.

At the primary level, students know addition and subtraction symbols in maths. They apply their knowledge when they use the symbols to solve equations.

Or they understand what a magnet is and move a puppet they have designed across a board using a magnet underneath and out of view.

Mobilisation is the active use of knowledge, and I want to unpack two main kinds.

The first kind has a predictable outcome and closed-ended mobilisation. The second is open-ended mobilisation. For knowledge to be mobilised, several elements must be activated and work together to achieve a goal.

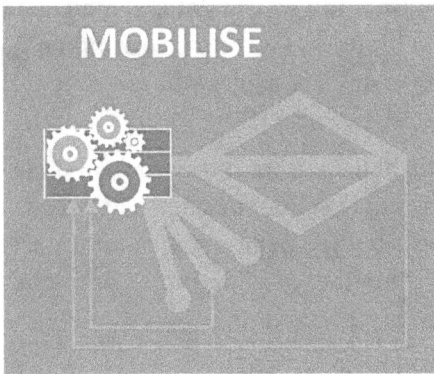

Figure 5: Closed-ended and open-ended mobilisation

Predictable or closed-ended mobilisation

Predictable mobilisation is when we use the information towards a known goal. This is usually done when specific information needs to be mastered and used during application tasks. Once a child has learned a new idea or unit of work, you might provide exercises or arrange materials to achieve a task. Children learn about balance, and they learn how to make things balance. Solving maths problems, using heat to melt ice, using a plan to write an essay. In all these scenarios, knowledge is mobilised, but we know what we are trying to achieve. If we are doing a jigsaw puzzle or solving a crossword, we need to activate several kinds of knowledge, but we know where we are going with it.

Problem-solving with a predictable outcome is not necessarily easy. It can be anything from simple to extraordinarily complex. Problem-solving, like comparison, uses a small set of subskills.

We have to:

- Define the problem
- Harness or develop a procedure for solving it
- Gather all the pieces of information
- Plan the process
- Manipulate the parts or steps to achieve the result
- Prioritise the steps in a sequential order
- Go through the procedure and reach a solution or conclusion

This is more than connecting knowledge; it is using it as a vehicle to reach a new product or destination. In some tasks, the sequence of the steps is more important than it is in others. You can't put a cake into an oven until the batter is mixed; but you might assemble a model aeroplane in several non-sequential steps towards the concluding step. Sometimes the steps are reversible: I can undo a jigsaw puzzle, but I can't unbake a cake. (Actually, I can't even bake a cake!)

An example here might help as we move from predictable to open-ended mobilisation. As a primary school teacher, you will have taught addition, subtraction, and possibly the beginnings of multiplication and division. Predictable mobilisation has you develop 12 problems for your students using the operations just covered.

Next, to ramp up the challenge and use an open-ended mobilisation, you set a challenge to find 17 ways that 17 is the answer. This problem is so widely opened that you would not possibly be able to predict everything your students come up with. Some might stick to addition and add up different numbers. Others might use a combination of all the operations. If you are lucky, some of them will bring in knowledge you haven't taught yet, surprising everyone. Open-ended mobilisation is the bridge to creativity.

Open-ended mobilisation

Many times in life, we act with no precise or known outcome. We must harness our current knowledge and use our best assessment to project or imagine what might happen. This kind of mobilisation can go in many directions, with different possible outcomes. But we still need a process to activate our intention.

Like problem-solving, in open-ended mobilisation, we will have some goals in mind. Usually, we visualise or imagine what we are trying to solve or achieve. Even if we are feeling our way, like selecting a fabric, we track what we feel to decide. We use our experience to develop a process. We use thinking skills like hypothesising, imagining, modelling, evaluating and creating.

Hypothesising using 'if-then' thinking

As an educator, you would like this hypothesising to elevate thinking. Ideally, you don't know the exact answer – it is something to be verified or discovered. Most human scientific investigation is based on hypothetical thinking.

It is not an accident that this kind of thinking is seen as high-order thinking and is usually at the top of any knowledge taxonomy, including the well-known and enduring Benjamin Bloom's taxonomy (Guskey, 2001), the revised Bloom's taxonomy (Anderson et al., 2001), and the work of John Biggs and Kevin Collis on Solo Taxonomy (Biggs, 2016). In Biggs' and Collis' work, this high-order inventiveness is called the *extended abstract*. When I read it I always imagine a figure at the edge of Earth's sphere, holding out a butterfly net – trying to catch the stars. So I had an amazing artist, Iulian Thomas in Romania, on a platform called Fiverr, draw it for me – and for you!

Nobel nominee and cognitive psychologist Reuven Feuerstein also created a comprehensive taxonomy of 28 cognitive functions categorised under input, elaboration and output (Feuerstein et al., 1980).

Figure 6: Child pursuing knowledge – extended abstract

I think that primary school children will use high-order mobilised thinking, but you might ask, 'Do preschool children do this?'

I spoke about the fairy incursion earlier, which was based on a playground conversation I had with a child during outdoor play. (The conversation later developed into a research project with the group.)

I was sitting on a bench and a child came and stood directly in front of me, eye to eye. (This is an object lesson in itself. I don't think she would have done it if I had been standing at that time.) She said, 'Mrs Wriggler.' (Translation: Kriegler, and yes, we did use the formal surnames!)

'Mrs Wriggler, I was thinking about making some wings. I was imagining my sewing machine... and my wings will have some web patterns on them.' Then she was quiet for a minute, looking at my upper body and shoulders, and continued: 'I can't lend you them.' Quiet contemplation... 'But I can make you some. I will need a *much* bigger sewing machine.' Then she turned and skipped off on her tiptoes, fluttering her arms and humming to herself.

Astounding. Not only had she combined and mobilised several sources of information about how to make wings, but she had worked out what she would have to do to adjust her project to accommodate my dimensions! She mentally compared sewing machines' size, shape and functionality to compare focus A and target B entities. She had recognised a problem, used all the pieces of information at her disposal, applied logical reasoning and hypothesised that a giant sewing machine was just the ticket!

Later that day, my co-teacher and I asked her to explain her ideas to her peers in a group meeting. We wondered whether she would like to try and make some wings the following day. She thought that was a grand idea. Other children got excited and it launched a project about wings of so many different kinds: birds, butterflies, fairies, dragons and mechanical wings for planes and rockets, among others. Her wings stretched into zoology, fantasy, engineering and science.

Mobilised, high-order thinking is definitely at home in the kindergarten.

Figure 7: Dragon wings – Joshua, four years old

Linking back to a sense of agency

After the discussion in the first three sections of this chapter, a predictable conclusion might be that you see knowledge mobilisation as much more important than static knowledge. In the last decade or so, much has been written and discussed about content knowledge not being that important, and that the emphasis should be on the process.

People will also say that the process is more important than the product. I am a great believer in the process, but I'm also a great believer in content and product.

At the 12th International Conference of Thinking (ICOT) in Melbourne in 2005, I was excited to attend an address by the leading expert on creativity, Edward de Bono. He raised the point about how educators value content versus process. He said that content was highly necessary for creativity. When creating, you consciously, or in a wonderful unconscious AHA moment, put together two disparate elements in a new relationship. A new idea, solution, humorous comment or illumination occurs. He indicated that the more children know, the more likely they are to be able to generate creative ideas. De Bono calls traditional knowledge vertical knowledge, which he sees as 'effective but incomplete' and must be supplemented with the 'generative qualities of creative thinking.' He states: 'There is no antagonism between the two sorts of thinking. Both are necessary. Vertical thinking is immensely useful, but one needs to enhance its usefulness by adding creativity and tempering its rigidity' (De Bono, 1998, p. 7).

De Bono's statements and the discussion above show a close relationship between static and mobilised knowledge, that they fuel each other. When we know and use information, we gain experience and skills. We reach a new platform. We can take on a more complex challenge from that new launching point. *But we can't go from zero to full throttle without fuel.* When we say that we need to offer children open-ended activities to not negatively affect their creativity, we should also say don't put them in that situation without the knowledge or process needed to embrace and enjoy the challenge. Sir Ken Robinson considered the two in this way: 'Imagination allows us to think of things that aren't real or around us at any given time, creativity allows us to do something meaningful with our imaginations' (Robinson & Aronica, 2010).

In honour of the now-late Sir Ken's comments, how do you use your imagination and creativity?

> ***Process words:*** *applying, decision-making, organising, planning, problem-solving, logical reasoning, sequencing, prioritising, concluding, imagining, hypothesising, creating*

In summary

- Mobilised learning begins when we apply static knowledge in an organised way to reach a goal
- Mobilised learning can be either predictable or open-ended
- Predictable mobilisation can be generally seen as problem-solving
- Open-ended mobilisation is also goal-oriented, but the outcome is unknown and could have several pathways
- Both predictable and unpredictable mobilisation use a small set of skills
- Planning requires sequencing, prioritisation, the exclusion of irrelevant information, an enactment and a conclusion
- Even very young children are capable of high-order mobilisation of knowledge
- There is a strong relationship between static and mobilised knowledge, and the former is fuel for the latter

4. Communicate

Communication is multimodal

To some, it might seem strange to list communication as one of four separate headings about knowledge. But it is a unique kind of knowledge. It is the means to encode and decode information. It is the package, not the substance.

The goal of all our education efforts is that students will be able to express what they have learned and what they know, think, feel and imagine. Communication can be broadly categorised into two domains: verbal and non-verbal.

Verbal communication includes oral language, reading and writing. Non-verbal communication consists of all body language and gestures, and the expression of ideas through media, movement and materials.

Each type of communication has its own structure, alphabet and vocabulary. Simply put, for music, it is the composition, the melody and the notes. For dance, it is the form, the choreography and the steps. Whether through spoken language, painting, movement, sculpture, music or dance, we learn to recognise and respond to central conventions and elements, enabling us to understand the message being communicated. The systems for communicating knowledge are separate from knowledge. They are the means to encode and decode knowledge to share it.

If you are familiar with the internationally renowned educational philosophy from Reggio Emilia in northern Italy, you will know that Loris Malaguzzi (the progenitor of the philosophy) saw children as having a hundred languages for expressing themselves.

> *The child*
> *is made of one hundred.*
> *The child has a hundred languages*
> *a hundred hands*
> *a hundred thoughts*
> *a hundred ways of thinking...*

The poem emphasises the multimodal nature of communication. Communication is internal: in the mind and the emotions; and external: expressed with the voice and the body. The educators in Reggio Emilia talk about 'the expressive, the communicative and the cognitive languages'.

This is the perfect way to talk about communication. It emphasises the infinite ability of the human mind and body to create forms of expression that enable us to formulate and share our experiences and our understanding of the world.

Children express their knowledge using 'words, movement, drawing, painting, building, sculpture, shadow play, collage, dramatic play or music, to name a few' (Edwards et al., 1998, pp. 3–7).

In the early years, expressive languages should not be considered to belong exclusively to the curriculum area of art. Rather, this expression, using media, tools and materials, is the children's vehicle for engaging with the world to develop an understanding of what it is and how it works. When I outline the learning zones in later chapters, you will see how these expressive languages are used this way.

As educators, we talk about developing students' literacy, which usually refers to verbal communication – speaking, reading and writing. But children can become literate in all modes of communication.

The modes we use to communicate information and meaning are very diverse: concrete manipulative, photographic, pictorial, graphic, tabular, schematic, symbolic, verbal written, verbal spoken, gestural, postural, locomotor and digital. You are likely to add even more.

Students thrive when they learn to decode and encode the structure and elements of each.

For example, the tabular format is highly underestimated. Knowledge of what a column is and what a row is, how the flow of communication goes from left to right and from top to bottom is assumed, not often overtly explained and understood. It is key for understanding the x and y axes later in maths. (Of course, these table directions are not the same in all languages.)

There are also conventions when interpreting pictures in books; for instance, what is above a character is usually interpreted as being spatially behind it. Speech bubbles and thinking bubbles are different.

Decoding and encoding modes of communication

In general, the decoding of information arrives first.

Young children's language learning is exponential.

Most often, their receptive language is much stronger than their expressive language. It is essential to support and strengthen the progress from receptive to expressive language. We can do this in multiple ways, which will be explored in detail soon.

If you are yawning as a primary teacher at this point (I see you!), let me say that this is also true of older children when they are learning new things. It takes a child about 40 repetitions of a word in context before they have genuinely consolidated it. So, even with older students, we need to be aware of developing solid vocabulary, ensuring children not only understand it, but can activate and articulate it with the appropriate meaning in the correct context.

There is a big divide between receptive understanding and auto-expression of that understanding. Expressive language does not only operate in conversation with others, but it is also a stepping stone to children's self-talk, or what we call interior dialogue. Self-talk is a vital component in thinking and learning. Where do you do most of your thinking, planning and problem-solving? (And I'm not talking about in the car or the shower.)

When children articulate their knowledge, they are encoding. This is a higher level of skill than decoding. They must come up with and activate the words themselves. This activation of recall is a recognised way that memory is enhanced (Buzan, 2010).

A similar gap in skills occurs when children are learning to write. In the same way that receptive language is more advanced than expressive in young children, there is a huge gap between what an early primary student can *tell you* and what they can communicate in their *writing*. If we insist that students write down their ideas, and we don't also allow them to communicate their knowledge orally or non-verbally, we could miss out on about 80% of what they know or think. So, as we introduce children to a new mode of communication, it is good practice to allow them to continue using the one they already have a good grasp of in order to maximise their expression.

Once students learn the structure, vocabulary and alphabet of different modes, they can use or break the rules to generate unique and creative products.

Later, we will explore the excellent information on the top-level structures of language as explained by Benjamin Bartlett (Bartlett, 2003).

Process words: communicating, understanding, recognising, monitoring, assigning meaning, interpreting, decoding, encoding, articulating, expressing

In summary

- Communication is the vehicle for decoding and encoding information
- Communication is multimodal and can be divided into verbal and non-verbal areas
- Decoding comes before encoding in most cases
- Each mode of communication has its structure, vocabulary and alphabet

- These are the central conventions we learn to interpret and deploy that format
- We should continue to allow students to use a mode they are good at while they are learning a new mode
- Once children understand the modes and their structures, they can use them to encode their ideas in unique and creative ways

Exhale!

One takeaway from this chapter is that high-order problem-solving and creativity are built on good foundational knowledge. Another is that you only see what you are looking for; if you expand your horizons or sharpen your focus, you see more.

I hope you will have a deeper understanding of each foundational knowledge component to support your planning and students' learning.

For your convenience, I have included a summary of 12 thinking skills as an appendix to this book. (See page 181.)

What kind of foundational knowledge is your favourite?

What are three things you might do differently after reading this chapter?

Is there something you'd like to share with your colleagues?

Chapter 3
Vertical knowledge
Power up your curriculum GPS

> *'Would you tell me, please, which way I ought to go from here?'*
> *'That depends a good deal on where you want to get to,'* said the Cat.
> *'I don't much care where,'* said Alice.
> *'Then it doesn't matter which way you go,'* said the Cat.
> Lewis Carroll, *Alice's Adventures in Wonderland*

Thoughts on planning excellent programs

When you embark on a journey, you load coordinates into your global positioning system (GPS). Your destination determines the route. In this way, when you plan your curriculum, you will have a goal in mind. From reading this book, I indicated that my goal for you is to feel energised and secure in your knowledge when you plan, implement and assess your curriculum to support concept-based learning. This relates to my vision that all educators are agile and adaptive to get the most out of every learning situation.

Expert planning, implementation and assessment combine to make your communication clear and confident. Parents will trust you, education authorities will cite your work, and your centre will be a role model of excellence.

First, clear away any idea that planning comes first. High-achieving educators set goals before they plan. And goals originate from educational vision. What do you want your curriculum to achieve? Second, planning and assessment are not separate; they are intertwined. Planning is what you project into your context. Assessment is monitoring what happens once it's activated. Planning is not a one-off thing that occurs at the start, and assessment is not a one-off thing that happens at the end. It is a constant to and fro – a dialogue. Sure, you do substantial planning at the start and report at the end. However, once your plan is enacted, you constantly assess and relaunch it.

Up to now, the discussion has been about concept formation and metacognition, about what is happening in children's brains. But we haven't looked at the content more broadly.

You want children to experience a thinking curriculum. While in play, children constantly think, even if thinking is a kind of sensory monitoring. What will you offer students to animate their concept formation and thinking?

There isn't a curriculum document worth its salt that doesn't have statements like these:

- We value creativity and encourage children to be independent thinkers
- We offer a comprehensive program
- We care for your child in a nurturing environment
- We build on interests
- We reinforce essential concepts
- We offer a customised learning journey for each child
- Your child will become a thoughtful global citizen
- We value and respect diversity
- We develop a play-based learning program

As mentioned, the launching point of your planning is what your vision encompasses and what you tell parents you do.

This book is not about persuading educators to step away from their philosophy. If a play-based curriculum is what you believe in, then that is what you continue to provide. If your curriculum is called the 'young scientists' program and you favour a structured STEM-focused curriculum, then similarly, that is what you will do. You may favour a Maria Montessori or a Rudolf Steiner program. And there are several other philosophies developed by pivotal early years thinkers of their time that are well-established and highly regarded.

The information in this book is offered to support your own *conceptual and metacognitive understanding* of what you do every minute of every day. It is about you *always recognising the potential to catalyse learning.*

As an adaptive educator, you are constantly and actively making decisions. You recognise opportunities in any situation to propel or pivot learning. Propelling learning is powerfully continuing on the same course. Pivoting learning is shifting the direction either slightly or dramatically to use what is current for a related or equally important but adjusted goal.

I have often encountered the staff in a centre or school who can state their vision but may not know exactly how to translate and animate it in their everyday practice. What is a comprehensive program? What is a customised learning journey? How do children increase their understanding of the world within these visions?

Mapping the curriculum

Where does content come from?

Let's talk about subject areas or disciplines – what I have referred to as vertical knowledge. You might be mandated to, or choose to, include specific subjects in your curriculum. My wish for you is, rather than feel your curriculum is dictated to you, is limiting or overwhelming you, that you use it as a reference to choreograph and design it in your own way. Have a personal point of view. Own it. If you ensure your content across the year is from several disciplines, your work will be balanced and comprehensive. Include your passions. Bring everything you know and love to it. In Reggio Emilia, educators look for inspiration from various sources. They reference the work of engineers, architects, poets, artists and designers.

Use knowledge, interests and ideas that resonate with you as the stimulus for your design. Then locate your personal focus within the disciplines where they originate and belong. In its discipline, your interest and ideas will connect to an extensive reservoir of existing and evolving knowledge you can draw on. It is a point to research from and to plan from. Use it to stretch students' learning in that discipline and across disciplines. Something you find fascinating – an artefact, idea or piece of music – can be a motivation. It is the stone thrown into a pond that generates a knowledge ripple effect.

STEM and humanities

As a junior primary teacher, you will have relative certainty about your curriculum's disciplines and subject areas. As a preschool teacher, you often have free rein, and sometimes that breadth of possibility is frightening rather than liberating!

Selecting content is artfully done, bearing in mind the current abilities of the children in the age range you are working with.

Although knowledge increases in complexity throughout schooling, it is a mistake to see early learning as simple. At the start of my work in preschool, I held what I thought was a logical belief: that playing with concrete materials could teach children anything on Earth. If only children played with blocks, surely they would all be good mathematicians! After all, blocks teach them about length, weight, size, shape, colour, balance, density, volume, symmetry, stability and number.

Any book on the value of play will list this type of conceptual learning. I didn't realise that the learning I observed was often experiential. Some children learn directly as though by osmosis, and they might know what all those features are called, but often, children need mediation and facilitation to genuinely understand these concepts. As you saw earlier, knowing something is only the beginning. It needs to be connected, stored, mobilised and communicated.

What was missing in my original thoughts was that children had to move beyond the here and now to master concepts abstractly. They can learn something experientially, but if they aren't able to label it, think about it and transfer it somewhere else, the knowledge is not available for use.

A tiny landmark book, *Children's Minds*, had me refine my ideas. Written by a student of Piaget, Margaret Donaldson (Donaldson, 1984), it revolutionised my educational purpose. I needed to be concerned with children's language learning, abstract thought, laying down foundations, transfer of knowledge and innovative ideas. I wasn't only teaching for today, I was teaching for the future.

Beyond the early years, content becomes more abstract and complex, and the amount of information grows by orders of magnitude. Content is so vast these days that we throw our hands up. There's just too much; we can't teach it all. I am sure you have heard that in the 21st century, it's not important to memorise content because we can look up anything on the internet.

Let's pause and consider that.

I agree with David Epstein's comment in his book *Range* that 'You have people walking around with all the knowledge of humanity on their phone, but they have no idea how to integrate it' (Epstein, 2019).

Content is the conceptual understanding of how the world works. Understanding is not isolated, random, episodic facts. Understanding is connected facts. To deal with the huge explosion of knowledge, what is required is not Google; it is an internal structure for organising and locating knowledge in the human brain.

If it's not in the brain or across a few marvellous collaborating brains, it cannot be used to fuel problem-solving or creativity. The idea is to have stored concepts that connect to more and more general categories.

A bird falls in the category of Aves, along with other animals in the broader area of zoology. Zoology is part of the life sciences, which are part of the general sciences. When it is located, it can be cross-pollinated and integrated with other high-order knowledge. Google comes in when you know that some of your knowledge is missing, and you embark on research. That's when you reach out to that fantastic network, the World Wide Web. Find others who are searching for new answers like you and synthesise knowledge in new ways or invent new thinking and ideas.

Children need subject knowledge, and they also need to know how it is expressed or communicated. Every discipline, at its foundation, is about literacy. I have never, and I'm sure you haven't either, come across a subject where we don't encounter specialised knowledge.

Like learning to speak a foreign language, we need to learn to 'speak' maths, computer science, music, dance, law and every other subject. Each discipline also has its structural forms, vocabulary and alphabet. Many have specific units of measurement to provide precision and accuracy in their communication.

We can journey towards our curriculum destination, packing a trunk containing only one subject, or we can load a couple of disciplines to enrich the journey.

A meeting of paths

There is a dialogue about children developing fluid knowledge in the early years.

In the 21st century, hybrid knowledge is where innovation originates more than ever. Think of 3D animations in medicine (WEHImovies, 2020). Digital communication and science together make it possible for the medical world to see human and other life forms' cross-sections, systems and micro-details in a way that has never been possible before.

Interdisciplinary content is quite challenging to achieve higher levels of education because subjects may be taught in silos by different teachers. For their work to become transdisciplinary or multidisciplinary, they must actively seek to collaborate. An inspiring film, *Most Likely to Succeed* is about how this was done in a high school in San Diego, USA (Whitely, 2015).

In the early years arena, you can achieve this cross-pollination much more easily. When you plan your content, you have an excellent opportunity to integrate disciplines. If you understand each discipline, you can overtly choose the ones you want to harness and use together.

When I want to position content, I think of the traditional sciences and humanities.

We regularly see this vertical knowledge classification:

- Science
- Technology
- Engineering
- Mathematics
- The Arts
- History
- Languages
- Literacy
- Philosophy
- Law
- Ethics

How is the overview of disciplines useful to us?

In short, the list is STEM plus the humanities.

For balance, we plan a curriculum which includes knowledge from a range of disciplines and implement it at the appropriate level, remembering Vygotsky's zone of proximal development.

Schools generally calibrate how balanced their subjects are in their scope and sequence across year levels. But occasionally, I have seen children do dinosaurs or hatch chicken eggs three or four times during their early education. Children don't benefit from this repetition, unless the complexity is ramped up. Or you see subjects being avoided because they seem abstract or difficult for young children. What of law, philosophy and ethics? There are ways to include these hard topics in your work. After all, what are the rules in your classroom? Who made them? Are they fair? How do you make collaborative decisions? What happens when someone breaks them? What can you do as a group for others?

High-level questions as gateways to discipline knowledge

With such an array of content and many disciplines available, how do we make them accessible?

The International Baccalaureate Organisation's Primary Years Program (IBO, 2020) has masterminded accessibility by formulating simple but profound overarching questions that open gates to our listed disciplines. Its curriculum asks: Who are we? Where are we in place and time? How do we express ourselves? How does the world work?

I love a question as an entrance to knowledge because it suggests that we must research and act to reach answers. I think the overarching questions are valuable and highly flexible entry points to discipline knowledge, and we can immediately see how 'knowing who we are' prompts us to think about our personal, communal and cultural identity. 'Where we are in place and time' suggests geography, history and more. If your centre has a religious or philosophical framework included in its vision, you might frame a complementary overarching question to open doors to that understanding. It is important to state here that an overarching overriding question asking us to understand our identity relates to past, current and future perspectives. More and more, our curricula ask us to engage with who we and our students are as enactors and generators of the future.

Onboarding your co-travellers

So now you've chosen subject areas and selected concept-rich content you want to cover.

Early in my career, I was made to feel intensely incompetent when a new teacher arrived with 46 boxes of plans, materials and resources for all 46 weeks of the school year! I was rabidly jealous. She was SO organised! She had delivered the same curriculum for the past eight years and counting.

I have learnt a lot since then!

If you go ahead and enact your plan as it is, you are limiting its potential. Your students' role needs to be accommodated if you are genuinely interested in their reciprocity, motivation and interest.

With us, without us, or despite us, children are active learners who constantly construct their own theories about how the world works. If they are institutionally ignored, they learn that it's not worth the effort to offer a suggestion.

Some educators might counter this notion of attending to young children's theories citing that they are often incorrect, unscientific or, frankly, untrue. Of course, this may be the case. However, the intention is not to leave children with partial understanding or ignorance. Rather it is to help them accumulate evidence in the world around them to refine and develop their ideas through a series of provisional theories. By providing experiences and materials to challenge them and by offering media and methods for communication and ongoing dialogue, we journey with them to conceptual clarity and creativity. When we do this, we usually discover that they have perspectives, wisdom, or imagination we hardly believed possible.

Loris Malaguzzi said:

> 'All people – and I mean scholars, researchers and teachers who in any place have set themselves to study children seriously – have ended up by discovering not so much the limits and weaknesses of children but rather their surprising and extraordinary strengths and capabilities linked with an inexhaustible need for expression and realization.'

In the next chapter, I will discuss a project called Explorations that aims to unpack ways to integrate curriculum goals and plans with children's ideas, motivations, and discoveries.

For now, I want to turn to assessment.

Thoughts on assessment

How is the journey going?

You read earlier that planning is what you project into your context, and assessment is monitoring what happens once it's activated.

Pedagogy of listening

In 2000, I made my first of three study tours to Reggio Emilia. One of the lectures by Carla Rinaldi reframed assessment as 'a pedagogy of listening'

(Rinaldi, 2001). When I heard her address on listening, it was the first time I recognised my value as an early childhood educator. This was a transformational moment. Many of you will understand when I say that as an early childhood educator, our role is not understood and often belittled. We just play, do finger painting, sit on the floor and tell stories. You know what I'm saying. But Carla put me straight. For the first time I felt like a true professional with intellectual rigour and an equal with any other educator anywhere.

The listening she describes uses all the educator's intellectual and affective faculties, not just their ears. The pedagogy of listening is respectful, hears back, gives time, is multimodal, sensitive, reflective, curious, conscious of emotion, suspends judgement, and most movingly, 'removes the individual from anonymity'.

These ideas are much less declarative than anything I have written in this book. This makes sense because I can declare my own knowledge, as can you, and I know my plan; but I honestly never know what I am listening for from children until I hear it. I can *anticipate* much of what I will hear back from the assessment, but I know that I will always be surprised, excited, concerned, validated, stumped, humbled, amused, delighted and so much more. Because every child is unique! We *don't* know everything about them.

When I am assessing, I am listening for more than intellectual knowledge. I am observing the relationships children have with their peers and their levels of motivation. Perseverance is on my radar. Not that I would insist that a child stick to some tasks beyond where frustration kicks in, but I want to extend it over time. I am checking to see whether they rely on the same friends, materials and activities each day so I can slightly challenge that and introduce some flexibility. I am watching for independence in negotiating the room and how stable or variable moods are. How they deal with conflict. And I know that you are, too, when you are in the observer/evaluator role. These observations collectively cross several areas. They relate to what Art Costa (Costa, 2008) calls habits of mind, or what Daniel Goleman (Goleman, 1995) characterises as emotional intelligence.

We are listening so that we can answer these questions: 'Who are these children?', 'How are they thinking, discovering, acting, communicating?', 'What are their relationships with the group?', and 'How are they interpreting the world?'

We also ask questions about ourselves

When we ask these questions, we are searching or researching. As secure as we think we are in our knowledge, research is being open. Research is about the process of learning, relationships, seeing possibility, finding new meaning, seeing links, experiencing highlights, finding nodes of interest, unpacking values, surfacing beliefs, recognising change, feeling emotion and seeing how everything is resonating together.

'Hang on a minute, Lili-Ann,' I hear you say. 'This book is about concepts, and you are hammering on about emotion, motivation and resilience. Isn't that another book?'

It is crucial to state that if we want conceptual understanding, we *have* to be aware of emotion. I've already stated how Piaget and Reuven Feuerstein saw emotion and cognition as two sides of the same coin. This means that children can metacognitively review and understand their emotions, moods, energy and application to a task through a lens of thinking rather than feeling. If it is only feeling, they cannot understand or transform their behaviour. If it is a thinking lens, they have the scope to pause, reflect and review. Emotion and thought are both harnessed in great concept learning.

With all our senses and through both cognitive and affective lenses, we tune in to what is happening successfully and what is running well. Our evaluation enables us to change course if interest wanes or find new resources to keep learning on track. Occasionally, this alertness might mean we have to design a new destination. But mostly, it means discovering the most meaningful and engaging path for our students.

Finding optimal engagement is a tightrope between not scaffolding children's understanding of the world enough and inundating them with prescriptive ideas that don't motivate or inspire them. Evaluation, listening and assessing are what enable you to balance on the rope. In many seminars I've presented, teachers start thinking assessment is the hardest and most frustrating part of their role and end up loving it the most.

In Chapter 6, I will discuss taming your assessment avalanche by clarifying your focus and managing the capture, recording, storage and flexible use of your observations.

Orientation provides different points of view

When you use the knowledge GPS to map your balanced curriculum, you must be aware of differing points of view. In our role, we deal with many vying stakeholders: government, education departments, leadership, colleagues, parents, students, specialists, the broader community and... the media. There will be disparate and even opposing points of view.

You will, hopefully, be guided by the vision and philosophy of your school or centre regarding how it positions itself. No matter what you include in your curriculum, you will be cognisant of these points of view and apply considerate filters. As educators, we are subject to social, ethical and philosophical dialogues around inclusion, culture, religion, family circumstances and gender.

Some educators and even organisations make sensitive topics the content for children. I don't believe it is their place. Rather, I recommend approaching content in a way that respects and honours diverse perspectives. Deliver content through a sensitive lens that is mindful and respectful of various points of view. Create a more inclusive learning environment without overtly influencing children's belief structures through your own perspectives or activism.

In summary

- It is helpful to have an overview of the disciplines from which our curricula are drawn and designed
- There are two overarching categories: STEM and humanities
- All the disciplines are underpinned by language and literacy
- Overarching questions are gateways or access points to subject areas
- We need children to experience a balance of disciplines over time, so a scope and sequence is desirable
- Assessment is the art of listening with all senses and with both intellect and affect to what is running well and to noting what children are learning, how they are interacting in social engagements and how they navigate the educational environment
- We need to ensure we are respectful of cultural, ethical, religious and gender issues

Chapter 4
Distributed knowledge

I therefore suggest that we should focus on the greatest source of variance that can make the difference – the teacher.
John Hattie

We looked at foundational, vertical and distributed knowledge in Chapter 2. I want to revisit it here to demonstrate vertical and distributed knowledge relationships. Vertical knowledge is what the world knows, and distributed knowledge is how we engage with that knowledge to adapt and advance it. You will note that when you plan content, you draw knowledge from different disciplines in the vertical knowledge domain. So this graphic is titled transdisciplinary knowledge. How you deploy and elaborate that knowledge with children is up to you. You set its energy, democracy, depth and range.

You will note the representation in the distributed knowledge domain of the closed- and open-ended systems. These have already been prefigured and will be discussed further.

I started by discussing three kinds of knowledge because I wanted to make sure you understood them. But notice here a fourth kind: cyclical knowledge.

Current vertical knowledge does not remain static. We are responsible for transforming what is known through our own learning, research, innovation and action. What we discover feeds back into vertical knowledge. There is also a relationship between closed- and open-ended systems. We and students use what we know to fuel creativity, and creativity gives us new formulas and rules to develop improved closed-ended systems. The following section discusses how traditional vertical knowledge fuels the curriculum. How is it investigated in closed- and open-ended formats. And how, as it is advanced, it becomes innovative distributed knowledge.

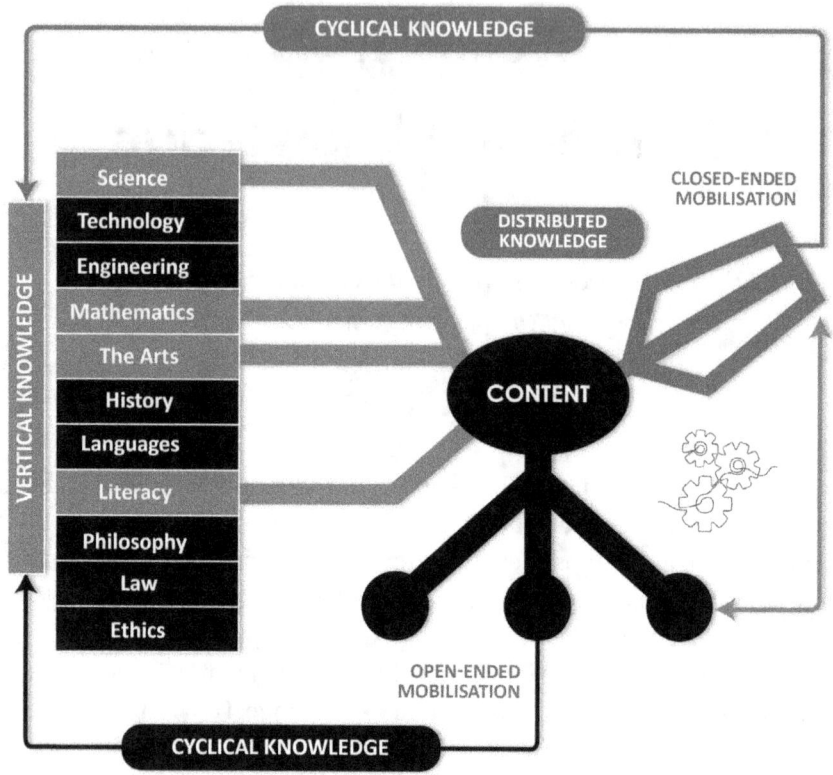

Figure 8: Transdisciplinary learning

The dancer and the dance

I've used the image before of you as the choreographer of your curriculum.

As a choreographer, you arrange the dance. But you also give over the dance to the dancers.

I said that I would share in this chapter the Explorations project to get a picture of how children's interests are included within your plan authentically.

I chose this project to discuss with you because it originated in a middle school setting as a collaborative exploration of the four elements: earth, fire, water and air. The Year 5s were in a 'buddy' program with the preschool where I was the director, teaching a group of four-year-olds three days a week. I loved the 'explorations' idea and was inspired to mirror it in our centre. The content is suitable for both primary and preschool students. The Year 5s did all four elements, and we chose 'air' for the three-year-olds and 'water' for the four-year-olds.

Dancing with projects

Our program was designed to include projects. But if you don't use a project-based methodology, you can still include some of these ideas in your setting. I am biased towards projects because of their strong integration of information and ideas across disciplines.

Projects can be long and transdisciplinary or short, sharp and limited in scope. You can reframe some of these ideas in a play-based environment without projects. An important point is that our program was not exclusively based on projects. We designed a learning environment you will recognise with a variety of play and learning spaces. Home or themed fantasy play corner, communication table, table-top activities, art easel, collage table, sand trays, inquiry displays, reading and book corner. Early primary classrooms often have the same flexibility and opportunities for large-group, small-group and individual experiences.

In the preschool setting, we usually have the fantastic luxury of two adults in the room. Over the years, I devised metaphors for our roles. During the day, one of us acted as a *microscope*, spending time with a small group for a purpose we had planned and resourced, and the other worked as *radar*, roving and documenting with photos or notes, directing, supporting, scaffolding, resourcing or observing the whole group. I particularly love the radar role because you are alert to what is emerging in the room as the children engage with one another and with materials.

To overcome the challenges of being a lone teacher, I have observed highly successful team teaching in primary settings, even though having two adults per group is uncommon. In some cases, two or even three teachers collaborate across a year level, planning together and assigning children to various activities across one or more spaces. This approach often ensures that at least one teacher is available to act as a 'radar,' providing support and oversight.

During projects, my co-teacher and I customised the room's arrangement to suit each project. Certain areas would be activated and resourced specifically to underpin the central ideas of a project. We didn't expect every child to be involved in the projects all the time; students naturally flowed in and out of them. For essential skills or knowledge, we created a list and ensured that every student engaged with a specific material or interpreted an idea. This approach often helped us gather data on their knowledge and skill development levels.

Sometimes we would start a project, pause, and then pick up the threads later. I was continually astounded by the children's incredible memory for these projects, especially how they remembered their own and others' contributions. One notable project I conducted across Prep and Year 1 involved children authoring collaborative books based on an author study of Leo Lionni. At that time, the teaching structure allowed me to have the same students for two years. When the children began their books, they couldn't read or write; instead, they told their stories orally and illustrated them. Two years later, at a book launch, they stood at a podium and read their books aloud to an audience of more than 80 parents and grandparents. Children truly have memories like elephants!

We planned two kinds of projects.

The Explorations project was about a single feature in the world: water. We took a single idea and broadened it out. At other times, our projects were more general, with titles like Taking Time, Body Talk, Our Place in Space and Line Dance, which explored how lines work in the world. In these projects, we started with a broad idea and explored what was within it. We always left space for mini projects, unrelated to the main project, to unravel into action.

Details of the Explorations project

After that meander into projects more generally back to Explorations.

When I decided to embark on Explorations, I did what I always do and developed a massive mind map of ideas related to water. I asked my colleagues to do the same. I was also interested in what parents and grandparents might bring to the project, so I sent out a newsletter and asked them if they were interested in sharing their ideas about what water meant to them.

I was inundated with responses.

Many of the ideas matched what we'd set out already, but there were some excellent new perspectives, like information about water engineering from a father involved in sanitation. We also included Indigenous perspectives, and during the project, an elder invited to our centre narrated some of the Dreamtime stories, including that of the Rainbow Serpent, who, in some versions, created waterways.

Among the disciplines included were:

- **Physics:** the states of water – liquid, solid, gas
- **Life sciences:** water as sustaining life
- **Geography:** landforms related to water, valleys, lakes, river systems, estuaries and the ocean
- **Urban planning:** water reticulation
- **The arts:** photography, painting, pen and ink drawing, narrative, drama, music and dance

Giving the dance over to the dancers

I will relate two stories which both harnessed children's interests. The first is about a 'water-moving machine'. I include it here because it is a situation where my colleagues and I had all the knowledge to solve problems for children but stood back and allowed them to do it independently. This is an instance of closed-ended mobilisation and problem-solving towards a predictable conclusion.

The second is about a 'water dance'. Here, once again, standing back was an excellent option. As you will see, the dance project is an example of mobilising knowledge with open-ended and unknown outcomes. We've talked about that as imagination and creativity.

The water-moving machine – closed-ended project

A child, Lewis, told me he wanted to make a water-moving machine.

'How amazing,' I said, 'do you know what it will look like?'

'Yes,' said Lewis.

He wanted to move water from one side of the sandpit to the other. The equipment available in the sandpit included two plastic PVC pipes about 1.5m in length with different diameters, so one fit inside the other, but not snugly.

Lewis laid them out in the sandpit, one partially inside the other, collected a bowl of water and tried to pour some into one side of the two-pipe structure. Of course, trying to pour water into pipes horizontal to the sand, with one cylinder being wider, was hopeless, to put it mildly.

Several children got involved in the problem-solving. They also had trouble trying to pour water into the pipes. The water was dribbling out at the entrance to the pipe and being absorbed into the sand at the source.

Just before the end of play, one child said, 'We have to lift it!' (Conceptual breakthrough!)

Inside the classroom, Lewis shared his plan and his problems. We suggested that anyone interested could draw the machine. The child who'd suggested raising the pipes drew them slanting down from a big wooden reel she knew we had in the garden. The concepts involved here relate to position and direction. The pipe had to be placed at an incline to ensure the gravitational downward flow of water.

Another child, whose mind had been ticking over, showed us he'd drawn the water being poured into the 'machine' with a watering can. This addressed the conceptual problem of dimension. The children had been trying to pour water into the mouth of the pipe using several less accurate vessels, and water was spilling before entering the pipe. They agreed the watering can was much better than the ineffectual bowl they had been using. They used these conceptual improvements to refine their drawings.

The next day, we marched out to the sandpit with a mission. The children had assembled all the equipment. But it wasn't plain sailing. They encountered issues keeping the pipes on the big reel. They also had to lock the inner pipe into place by pushing some cloth between it and the pipe containing it. They had to bolster the two-pipe unit up halfway along (concept of stability.)

Eventually, after multiple attempts, the watering can poured water along the slanted pipes to the other side of the sandpit. Gravity, inclines and managing flow had worked for them. After all that, the water was seeping into the sand at the opposite end! They had to figure out a way to collect the water. A plastic container was produced in a brainwave, and the supplier explained that it didn't leak because it wasn't 'sorbent' like the sand.

Through a combination of planning, experimenting, drawing and refining the drawings, the children solved several conceptual physics problems. It couldn't be explained verbally from the start. When the originator of the idea and his friends drew and reflected on the problems, they could progress the solutions. The machine's efficiency was developed using different modalities, such as concrete manipulation, thinking, drawing, and trial and error. The children were on the verge of explaining the concept of 'pressure' because they knew the flow needed to be constant for the water to continue moving through the pipes. This was a short project integrating different sources of knowledge.

Figure 9: The water-moving machine

Water dance

One day, when we were still involved in the Explorations project, Matilda showed up with a program from *The Nutcracker* ballet.

How would you respond?

You could honour her interest by engaging in a brief conversation and acknowledge her generosity in sharing it with you. Or you might give her time to tell the group about it and ask her to place it on an investigation table.

Park it?

You can keep it parked – and sometimes, that is the best decision. To follow the lead of children's interests, you need to expend time and effort, which are finite commodities. You need to ensure that if you progress the idea, it has value for her, the individual child, and the group.

Do you decide to use it to elevate children's learning? And how do you do that?

The ballet program is an artefact. It is located in performance arts and is also a specific communication format. How do you include the artefact in your curriculum?

Do you consider what else the ballet program can be connected to? Perhaps there will be a multicultural celebration soon, and the famous national dances in *The Nutcracker* dovetail into the planning for that.

In my case, the Year 5 students happened to be creating a 'Water Dance' on the middle school campus as part of their exploration. So, I organised for them to come across and perform it for our groups. Our students immediately wanted to do their own dance.

As stated, the ballet program links to performance arts and literacy. But why stop at two disciplines? This is the secret of transdisciplinary learning. The children began. They liked the idea of a water dance, but it had to include the hip-hop 'worm' some of them were obsessed with. No pirouettes. Surprise! Not everyone is a balletomane like me!

The children spent time experimenting and devising their steps for the dance. There were many flowing waves and spirals, and the worms were water droplets popping into a pool. We provided photographs of different patterns of water, like concentric circles, waves, droplets, etc. These photographs were also the source of some exceptional water pattern paintings. I have a digital montage of them displayed in my home! I have included four of them here, because they suggest the dance steps the children created for their dance.

We resourced the children with time, space, writing and art materials to represent the dance.

It was not a drawing of dancers.

They invented a symbol system for each step and recorded the sequence of steps. Then, they recorded how many repetitions each sequence had in the structure. They negotiated. They assigned roles, refined the choreography, practised, organised the costumes, created a program, invited everyone, planned the seating, planned the menu and finally got to perform for an audience of parents.

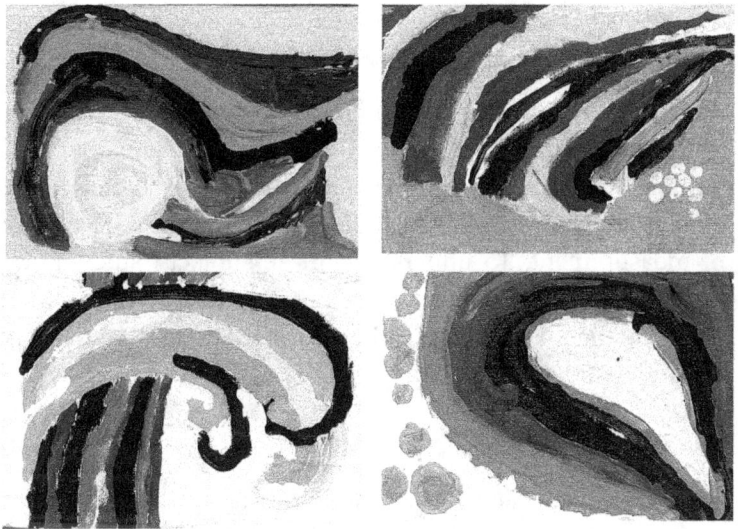

Figure 10: Water pattern paintings – four-year-old children

The artefact mobilised open-ended creativity. By the end of the project, the children had used formats and units of measurement from literacy, geometric and numerical mathematics and the performance arts. Their agency was intact, and there was tremendous collaborative planning and action. These are all things we are counselled to ensure children are capable of when they navigate the world in the 21st century.

It is no accident that the students created a symbol system for their dance or counted the sequences in the structure to record them. Much of this was choreographed by asking them questions, providing materials and asking refining questions. Children don't have to be told what to do; they can respond to scaffolding, finely tuned prompts and facilitation.

Communicating ideas

What was my purpose in having the children represent their ideas using their own diagrams and symbols? It was so that they themselves encoded information into modes that could be interpreted by others. Did their Uncle Ed understand the symbols? Most likely not, but *they* did. They had agreed on what the symbols meant.

And that is what is happening in the world in all disciplines all the time. People agree about what signs mean. Even as we invent new technologies, like digital modes and coding, the languages must be precise and communicable. For instance, in maths, there is this squiggly sign: π.

Laying down foundations for later learning

Each discipline has specific content, but it also has characteristic universally agreed-upon formats and modes of communication. Literature has poems; maths has equations; science has experiments; dance has pas de deux and pirouettes... and worms! Some disciplines also have definitive units of measurement. To understand these subjects, students will be required to master specialised forms, symbols and terminology. When the children create their own symbols, they learn about multimodal communication. And their learning is active, not passive.

When do you serve your pi?

As early childhood educators, we are building the foundations of learning. It helps if we know where children are going on their academic journey. In the example of pi, I show how we can teach parts of complex concepts when children are in preschool. Then, when they encounter the more complex ideas later, the simpler ones are already consolidated.

I often call this the three-hat idea. As an educator, your work will be more impactful if you wear three hats. You understand where children have been conceptually, where they are now and where they are going.

Pi is one of the most well-known mathematical constants representing the ratio of a circle's circumference to its diameter. For any circle, the distance around the edge, the circumference, is slightly more than three times the distance across, the diameter. Pi, 3.141592654, is one of literally hundreds of symbols children must learn to interpret and remember as they navigate the subject. At an appropriate year level, they must have a conceptual understanding of the symbol (π).

We are not going to teach pi in preschool or early primary, but length is a component of understanding pi. And preschool children can easily explore length. Children can use string to surround a circle, cut it and unwind it. It's a reference and can be compared to the string from a bigger, equal or smaller circle. Pi can't be understood without this first step – measuring the circumference of a circle. (We don't use the word 'circumference', but be ready for the child who might!)

To understand pi, children must also know what a diameter is. And a ratio.

Ratio and proportion, *without using the terminology*, can be investigated with a wide range of hands-on experiences in the early years. Understanding 'more', 'the same' and 'less' is what we are always doing in mathematics.

'Look at the water in this glass; I wonder, if we pour it into that jar, will it be more than half or less than half?'

'I wonder which block weighs more?'

'Oh, you have discovered that the big block weighs the same as these two blocks together! So, we need two blocks on one side of the scale to balance the big block there. It's two small to one big. (2:1) What if we have two big blocks?'

We don't serve pi up too early, but we begin to develop the *foundational understanding* so that later, they are the kids who get it.

When you do geography, you must understand how to represent topography or weather systems. Again, I'm not suggesting that you teach every child isobar and contour lines! Contour lines are interesting because the closer they are together, the steeper the slope they represent. We don't teach it, but perhaps, as for the water-moving machine and water dance, we offer children the opportunity to create their own drawings to represent steep and not steep. If they invent ways to represent their ideas, theories and concepts in drawings, diagrams, maps, plans, models, measurements and symbols, it tunes them in to how they will encounter knowledge later. It enhances our agility if we consider the kind of multimodal communication contained in different subjects. Children are not there yet, nor do they need to be. But they are moving towards it.

Early individualistic representation will give way over time to more universal formats, symbols and units, which are introduced to them in their schooling. They might even discover for themselves that communication is useless unless everyone understands it. Or that you can't use something arbitrary to measure with precision.

There is a book about a pivotal project from the Diana School in Reggio Emilia called *The Shoe and the Meter*. It explores the process preschool children go through to reach an agreed unit of measurement when they discover that different shoes do not measure things precisely enough (Castagnetti & Vecchi, 1997). The project is a negotiation and exploration about understanding the importance of universally agreed units. The actual brass metre referred to in the book can be visited in the city of Reggio Emilia.

I hear you saying that if you waited for children to create their own units first or discover everything in the world on their own all the time, you'd go nuts! And I agree! *You can't do it all the time.* But when you are planning, where can you fit it in so that they have the idea, the frustration, the challenge, the discussion, the negotiation and the steps to reach a solution?

And when, in your incidental interactions with children, can you frame things as a wandering or a brief investigation rather than as an answer?

What are your three takeaways from this chapter?

Is there an idea that particularly appealed to you?

What might you try in your context after reading this chapter?

In summary

- We can integrate learning from more than one discipline when we design content
- We can work from an individual artefact to the discipline, or work from the discipline, through sub-content to ideas and artefacts
- Each discipline has its unique structure, concepts, vocabulary, alphabet, and often, units of measurement
- Children benefit from encoding their own ideas and concepts in multi-modal ways as a means of recording their own ideas and concepts
- Curriculum engages children when we honour and authentically integrate their interests for the benefit of the individual child and the group

Chapter 5

Concept transfer

Crossing the bridge

An individual understands a concept, skill, theory, or domain of knowledge to the extent that he or she can apply it appropriately in a new situation.
Howard Gardner (Gardner, *The Disciplined Mind*, 2000)

I am sure you wish that one day your students will say that they learned many important things from you. An AHA moment, an insight, an inspiration, or even better, a string of them made a difference in their lives. The best knowledge is a thread that endures and stays the course through upheavals and transformations.

As I wrote the first edition of this book, our family was in lockdown. We were in the middle of the global COVID-19 crisis. Three of us were in Victoria and one was interstate, unable to fly anywhere. We Victorians were restricted in travel with a limit of a 5km radius and a 9pm curfew. In my whole life, I never anticipated this situation. We have had to adapt our expectations, relaunch our ways of communicating, imagine new ways of connecting emotionally and design new ways to enact our professional roles. We must take what we know from the situation before, adapt and redesign. Taking what we know from one context and adapting it to suit a new context is a transfer. Without it, we would have a hard time dealing with change. And we know that the only certain thing about life is that it will change.

Transfer is a key goal of successful teaching

As referred to earlier, with the explosion of knowledge, we need to find an approach that enables students to 'use their knowledge across situations' (Darling-Hammond et al., 2008).

In any course about education, we are trained that 'transfer' is an important goal to achieve. Students need to internalise the information we are presenting, and then be able to leverage that information elsewhere.

This is much more difficult and complex than it sounds. Unless we structure our teaching to focus on and demonstrate transfer, only some students will do it. Some students can think laterally and apply what they know in different contexts, but not all students do it. It can't be left to chance.

Transfer implies that a student understands something in a current situation and perceives how it is related to other objects and situations. Or they are in a novel situation and can import information or skills from a former situation to a new one. Their knowledge is built from a conceptual understanding. They understand patterns and relationships and can apply them across many contexts and disciplines.

Learning to understand relationships in depth facilitates subsequent transfer (Darling-Hammond et al., 2008, p. 7).

There are two kinds of transfer depending on how similar the tasks are:
1. **Near transfer:** transfer of knowledge between similar contexts.
2. **Far transfer:** transfer of knowledge between dissimilar contexts.

The first step in facilitating transfer is for children to develop a deep and complete understanding of something in its original context. If the initial learning, particularly if it's something a little complex, isn't consolidated, there is less chance that they can have it available as a reference point in a new context. Deep knowledge, structural knowledge, not surface knowledge, facilitates transfer (Meadows, 1993).

A motif throughout this book is that organising knowledge is important. When we do this, we take something in the immediate here and now, like me typing on this computer, and link it to other things to contextualise this activity. I am engaged in a recognised convention for communication. Take children learning about the plus sign. If they don't learn precisely what the plus sign represents, they are limited to using it to do the specific sum they are working on at that specific moment. They need to go from the particular to the general.

This difference between the specific and the general is something you know well. But even if we educators realise it, we might not plan for it to happen.

Spend time at the entrance to the bridge

Learning something new involves a process. One secret is to ensure that the first contacts are long and deep enough, and that there isn't interference while it is being learned.

A prompt here is that this information will be very relevant later when you read about the zone of concept clarity.

When working with children, I have made the error of simultaneously introducing the terms 'vertical' and 'horizontal'. I thought it would be simple because they both refer to positions in space, and I assumed kids couldn't possibly confuse standing up and lying down. They didn't confuse the positions, but they did confuse the terminology. 'Hold up your hands to the ceiling. What do we call this?' Half the kids yelled 'vertical!' the other half yelled 'horizontal!'

Uh oh.

Present information bytes on their own first. Consolidate. Next, before going on to the opposite or different information, provide bytes that are the same or partially similar. Even if elements are different, *concentrate on what is the same as the original byte* in the new information field. Once that is done well, then select to focus on difference.

Andreas Hansen, in his work on concept-based learning, presents a three-part process for learning a new concept (Hansen, 2014):

1. **Selective association:** concentrating on what is the same or similar
2. **Selective discrimination:** concentrating on what is different
3. **Selective generalisation:** knowing the concepts so well that you can focus on several similarities and differences in a complex field

I will use the introduction to the concept of a rectangle to explain this process, but you can substitute any concept for the rectangle. 2D linear shapes are fairly easy to grasp, but imagine introducing fractions. You will see through the process below that for fractions, sticking to one concept, like a half, will be better than trying to introduce too many fraction variables at the same time.

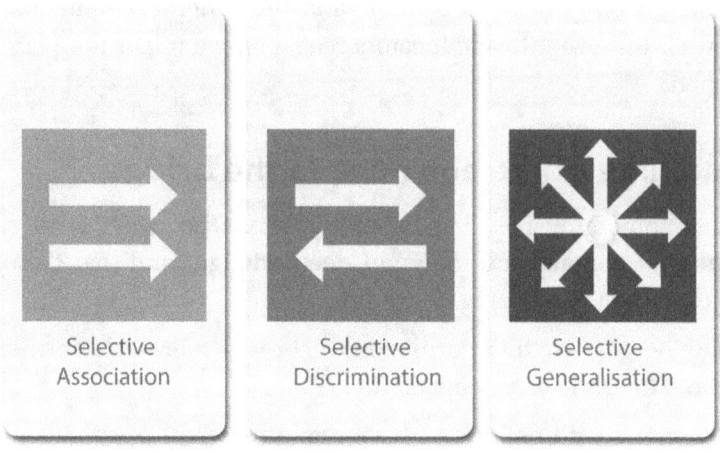

Figure 11: Three phases of concept learning

Selective association

Selective association, the first kind, is the one you spend the most time on, and it has three stages:

1. **Stage one:** The first is genuinely understanding the entity you're introducing and its features. Spend time unpacking them with children and supplying them with the appropriate language and labels. So if we introduce a rectangle, you will talk about the *number* of sides, the *shape* of the *angle* or the corners, and the *straightness* of the lines. The italicised words refer to the features.

2. **Stage two:** During the second stage, you compare the focus entity to other things with the same or similar features; *but stay in the immediate context first.* You slightly broaden the concept within a close transfer field. For example, you arrange some rectangles on the desktop from your box of beautiful tessellation shapes. Children are asked to find the exact match. When they can do this, they might be challenged to find one a different *colour*, or *size*, but still a rectangle.

   Then, explore the concept in the classroom. (Not all on the same day, necessarily.) Look at illustrations and 3D blocks, pointing out the rectangles. (Don't call the 3D block a prism yet.) The rectangle is partially similar because it is a 2D rectangular face of the 3D block.

As part of the second stage, you will ask children if they know where rectangles might exist beyond what they can see. Where are there rectangles in your home?

'I know, my fridge!'

'My front doormat.'

'Hazelnut chocolate bar.' (No, they did not say that.)

'The back flap that lifts on my yellow dump truck, which goes with the digger and the concrete mixer.'

These images challenge them to create a *mental picture* of the shape and fuel their ability to transfer the concept in the future.

3. **Stage three:** The third stage of selective association involves having children create their own examples of the concept. As we have seen, self-production is about encoding. This can be very creative. You might ask the children to start a drawing with a rectangle and then turn it into something else or provide collage materials with rectangles of different sizes to create a design. This can be done so they work out that four small ones make up one big one, etc. You can do rectangles outdoors or create human rectangular formations, etc.

   You will know your students have got it when a parent says, 'I had no idea there were so many rectangles at my house and the supermarket! Now his kid sister is collecting them, too!'

After selective association, you go on to selective discrimination. But also, do not go too far too soon.

Selective discrimination

When introducing the first difference from a rectangle, introduce a square shape that still has right-angled corners and straight lines. Emphasise the number of lines, the length of the lines and the shape of the angles. When they understand these features, the road is open to triangles. You can later revert to the rectangle and broaden the discussion to quadrilaterals, where the corners are not right angles. Try to introduce the logical next challenge.

Young children may not know what a right angle is or understand 90°, but they can learn to recognise this specific corner visually. You might join two strips of paper with a split pin and allow them to walk around the room, opening the angle of the two strips to match corners on the edge of tables, etc. Then, estimate if they have guessed it right and check their estimation.

So, deep understanding is fully understanding something's features and how they change from one universal shape (or other concept) to another.

If they know about a pentagon and it's called that because of its five corners, even if they don't know the name for an octagon yet, they might be able to provide a near-accurate name: an 'eightagon' perhaps. They understand the *constant structural ideas* across different examples. Some elements remain the same, such as conservation of constancy, and some change. And the children can identify and track both.

Selective generalisation

Once students understand the conservation of constancy of a particular feature, they will be able to work out similarities and differences across various contexts. They can choose, in any context, what is similar or different and to what degree.

So the idea is that when we learn a new concept, we go through this sequence:

1. Label and understand the features of an entity within a context
2. Relate it to identical entities or those with partial similarities in the immediate context
3. Extend the transfer field to more general instances of the concept within a near locale
4. Predict or imagine the entity in a place beyond the locale and where it is not accessible to the senses
5. Encode the entity in self-production tasks
6. Distinguish how the feature changes in another example
7. Be able to recognise similarities and differences in focal features in a complex field

When we have mediated children through association, discrimination and generalisation, we can challenge them to recognise, categorise, compare, export, reapply and create using their detailed understanding of concepts. You can mix it up. That gives them the practice they need to identify, apply and activate the concepts elsewhere – transfer.

As stated, I have used a maths example: the rectangle. This process for concept acquisition is equally valid for a writing format, a punctuation mark, a landform or a staccato. It is even more important when the content is complex. Fractions, decimals, percentages, ratios and proportions all have a structural foundation. They are all different ways of explaining part of a confined range, a whole.

In this range, 20%, one fifth, .2 and 1:5 are all related. If students understand the structural concept of proportion, they will have less difficulty seeing how these symbolic representations are proportionally the same.

Transporting principles across the bridge

Figure 12: Transfer of bridged concepts

Over the last ten years, I have become a trainer in Feuerstein Instrumental Enrichment (FIE) (Feuerstein Institute, 2020). That does not mean I have studied music! The instruments are aimed at clarifying particular cognitive functions. Feuerstein methodology packages transfer into every teaching engagement with students. At some point during each encounter, the teacher mediates students' thinking, and together, they come up with a generalisable *principle* from the learning.

For instance, the principle might be: 'for a shape to be a square, it needs four corners connected by four equal straight lines'. Or: 'If I focus well, I am more able to understand the task I am doing'. Or: 'If I face a different way, what is on my left and on my right will change.' Or: 'When I start a task, I must gather all the information.'

The first principle, or general statement, relates to content: the features of a square. The second principle of self-regulation is dispositional. The third reveals personal perspective in spatial relations, and the fourth emphasises that there are steps in a procedure and having all the data is step one.

When we create a universal principle, the information is generalised and readily packaged to be used in another context. It can be transported across a bridge. At home, the child is asked to go to a cupboard and bring back the square cake tin. They know exactly what to look for and don't return with a rectangular one.

When the student is in a different classroom with a different teacher approaching a task in a different discipline, they can say the mantra: 'If I focus well, I am more able to understand the task I am doing.' In developing this principle, they have been made aware of self-regulation and that it can be efficient or inefficient.

Without that awareness, they act out a pattern over which they have no conscious control. Recognising and being in touch with their feelings or attitudes towards learning is being mindful about it.

They might learn to think:

> *Sometimes, I don't focus well, but I am getting better at it.*
>
> *What helps me is to move away from my best friend in the classroom.*
>
> *If I imagine staying on a path and not going off it, I can concentrate for longer.*

Without mindfulness, students aren't alerted that their current state is not the only state available to them. When I was working with one student on self-regulation during my home consultancy, she suddenly grabbed her head to stop herself from looking around at my cat. She had become aware of her distraction, whereas before, she had no consciousness of it.

Exposure to the idea of mindfulness, where you have control over how you interpret a situation, can be a game changer for students. Without awareness of the possibility of adopting a different approach, students are locked into how they react to a situation. If students are not attuned to their sense of where they are, they will be locked into their current performance. Through skilful mediation, they can be encouraged to improve their ability by making different decisions, practising new skills or behaving differently.

The development of positive and productive mindsets is a metacognitive activity. I referred to this earlier in the image of emotion and cognition being two sides of the same coin. The difference between reaction and reflection can be between being stuck on one plane or stepping onto an upward spiral of self-actualisation and achievement.

How we respond to children's behaviour influences their beliefs about themselves. I was fortunate to learn one of my greatest life lessons one day from a colleague in the playground. A child had a broom and was about to whack someone with it.

Think about what you would have done.

My remarkable colleague swooped in and said: 'You are just the person I need right now. You have the broom. I have some sand, and I must have it cleaned up now. You're strong enough to be one of my best helpers.'

The genius of what she did was to use the words 'one of'. It meant that this child and any child in her hearing had a new idea of who and what they could be. The broom became quite popular that week!

Formulating the principle that has them decide the goal they want to work on is a step towards making students reflective. They understand they have a range of choices, rather than being simply reactive, where the options are invisible to them. For the soundest information on mindset, it is best to go to the work of Carol Dweck herself (Dweck, 2006). Mindfulness is conceptual.

Formulating a principle is an essential step in applying the learning process. Once the principle is packaged, the student is asked to think about where else they can use it. They are encouraged to suggest another place in the curriculum, at home or possibly on the sports field. They are often asked how their parents or siblings might use it to get the idea that it also applies to others. This way, transfer becomes an expected part of the learning process.

As educators, we always seek to develop students' capacity for three kinds of transfer: content, thinking processes and the positive intellectual attitudes or dispositions they attach to their thinking and learning.

Ron Ritchhart, the research associate from Project Zero, Harvard, indicates that the 'best and perhaps the ultimate thinking-infused program is a curriculum focused on understanding'. He quotes Jerome Bruner (Bruner, 1973). To define understanding, 'it is the ability to go beyond the information given, to use our skills and knowledge in novel circumstances and in the creation of new ideas.'

In summary

- Transfer of knowledge and skills is important for transforming expertise and adapting to change
- Transferred knowledge can be flexed for innovation
- Planning for transfer increases the likelihood that it will occur
- Transfer occurs as near transfer, similar in kind and context; or far transfer, where the context is dissimilar and removed
- The capacity to enact transfer benefits from learning to relate entities to others that are similar and proximal first; and then relating to entities that are dissimilar and distant
- Three kinds of transfer have been highlighted in this chapter: content, process and dispositional
- Deriving universal principles from specific events facilitates the packaging or information for more effortless transfer

Chapter 6
Avert the assessment avalanche

> *The best way to find out what we really need
> is to get rid of what we don't.*
>
> Marie Kondo

You arrive at work on a Monday morning refreshed and ready to go. You've spent time with your family, contacted a few friends, had a leisurely breakfast on Sunday and went to bed early after reading a chapter of your fabulous new book.

Said no teacher ever.

Dashing to school, bleary-eyed, trailing stuff, wondering how you're going to catch up on last week, let alone manage the new one. You tried to have time with your family, skipped over contacting friends, sent the kids to the park with somebody on Sunday (if you have kids, or a somebody) and spent the afternoon dealing with learning stories, portfolios, observations, checklists, updating the parent book, refreshing the new digital portal with a quick story and some photos… and Oh no, not again!, writing reports.

(Forgive me if I have made any assumptions about your lifestyle. I know that there are many different kinds of families worldwide.) But it is a metaphor for your relationship with your work. Of all the questions I get asked, 70% are about assessment and reporting.

Assessment, evaluation and reflection allow us to think critically and constructively about our work. They are all part of the process that helps us monitor and judge the success of the learning processes and how well students have internalised the information. It is the basis of all reporting.

Like planning, your assessment links directly to your vision. You've made the effort to consider many perspectives about early education. You may even have chosen where you work based on your internal belief systems, and your image of children. What specific knowledge, skills, emotional tone, competence, integration, curiosity, courage, flexibility, collaboration and types of play would you like to see? What are your place's precise features and conceptual building blocks?

Assessment is improved if you are focused on what you collect and curate. In this book, I hope to help you to look for conceptual understanding within your curriculum and record its formation and mobilisation in both closed- and open-ended interactions with peers and materials.

A school or centre might use some of Steven Covey's (Covey, 2013) amazing work to develop a mission statement encapsulating and manifesting their vision. Now you've chosen, design your assessment plan. Don't compare your context to everyone else. Different philosophies use different lenses, and you are looking for what makes your context unique, as it underpins your students' knowledge, wellbeing and social integration. Knowing what you want is half the battle.

Eight Ps for assessment and appraisal

In the Cambridge dictionary, appraisal is *'the act of examining someone or something in order to judge their qualities, success or needs.'*

I think this is a great definition because it assesses not only what is to be seen, but also what needs to be done in the next steps. We can employ the usual suspects: why, what, how, who and when.

Purpose

Why are you assessing? What are you looking for?

The very first thing to consider is what is prescribed. Is there a national, federal, state, municipal or school compliance framework, document, process or report you must attend to? If there is, plan for that first. It might even be outside how you want to report on your preferred process, but accept it. Combine capturing evidence of prescribed outcomes and capturing what relates to your vision. As much as possible, use the same systems you put in place to accomplish both. Streamlining is the best course of action.

Plan your desired assessment. Usually you're looking for social connection, emotional wellbeing, cognitive involvement, physical wellbeing, and if it's part of your vision, spiritual wellbeing.

Processes

No assessment or evaluation can occur without collecting data.

How are you going to do this?

You know what you want to collect and select the processes to do it.

Modern digital modes are extremely adaptable, and online planning, assessment and communication platforms can streamline your efforts by allowing you to have everything handy in one place.

Photography and video are useful, but don't underestimate the time and skill needed to organise, edit and track your digital collections. If you do use a digital platform, train everyone to use it and dispense with hard copies of everything. Ensure that technical support is available for digital processes to avoid time wasting and frustration.

There are many ways of recording data, and you should choose three to four ways that all give you different information. There are complex processes like the pedagogical documentation associated with the Reggio Emilia philosophy, but they should fit your vision and you have to be committed to them. If you are using them, you will research the techniques and eliminate any other kinds of assessments that don't belong in the process.

You can use learning stories, keep portfolios, use short anecdotal indoor and outdoor observations, and develop checklists for physical or cognitive skills.

A huge mistake is hearing about what someone else is doing somewhere else and rushing to include it. STOP! Either adjust what you are already doing, or if you genuinely think it is a better approach, then adopt it, *but throw out what it is replacing*. You've all heard that it's the last dump of snow that breaks the teacher's back!

Practicality

What can be expected of staff?

The vision and organisation you've already put in place make allocating roles much easier.

In my centre, my co-teacher typed up the early-morning and group discussions on a computer as we conversed with children. Prior to this incredible innovation, it all used to be written down and I used to type it up later. We used documentation of children's conversations and comments as part of our data collection. And when I was typing up what every child had contributed, and the sequence of the conversation, it made me think more deeply about their conceptual grasp of the content. Reflection after the fact often reveals new ways of interpreting what you heard in the moment – and may suggest possibilities.

As your read earlier in the preschool setting, we usually have the miracle of two adults in the room. During the day, one of us acted as a microscope, spending time with a small group for a purpose we had planned and resourced, and the other, as radar, roving and documenting with photos or notes, directing, supporting, scaffolding, resourcing or observing the whole group.

In both roles, we learnt what to document and what to leave out. It is not practical to take down everything, and neither is it necessary. What you look for is what adds to the current state of knowledge or emotional tone in your classroom. Nothing should ever be repeated or duplicated. Capture what has progressed or what can be used to move things forward.

We used a booklet outdoors with each child's name on a page. If we noticed something we were looking for or which surprised us, we would quickly date and note it down. If there were verbatim quotes from children, we took them down exactly as we heard them. Our children would repeat what they said for us and often even asked us to note down their ideas. These snippets might be done on an iPad and then added to the normal digital storage.

In the classroom, you can respectfully attach children's comments about their own artworks and products. If it's not practical to turn their work over and write on the back (the daffodils are dripping glistening globs of yellow paint) or tastefully write at the bottom of their drawing, attach a note with their comments. Their comments are inroads to their thinking, their own awareness of their skills, and a means to track how they connect and elevate their knowledge. It is probably a good place to say that with all the phenomenal new digital means, like photography, digital voice recording, video and sharing capacity, children can capture, assess and document some of their own process and products.

Progress

Never duplicate your data. I have seen observations where a particular child or group of children are described three times a week doing the same thing. 'John, Will and Evan returned to the sandpit today. They shared the dump truck they love and used it to build a sandhill.' If that returning is happening day after day, ask yourself why. Would you like to see them doing something else? If not, fine. But for your own sanity, don't write it down again. If you do want to see change, plan the means to move them up the spiral. Then document the progress. We want to track what, how and why things are changing. Focus on quality, not quantity.

Primary and secondary sources

When you collect your data, it is a primary source. You might have photos, a typed conversation, observations from indoors and outdoors and several checklists. Once you have the data, it can be repurposed for different requirements.

Photographs you collect both indoors and outdoors can be uploaded into a weekly digital group folder. Once there, you extract photos from the general upload into each child's individual digital folder. Online programs allow you to select a picture and tag it to another folder, so you don't have to recopy and use up memory space on your computer. You have a chronological tableau of what happened within the group. You also have a sequence of important documented information for each child.

We are really snap-happy these days! If I look at a photo and ask why it was taken, when it happened, how it started and what happened next, I haven't got the story. It's no use just having a finger on the trigger. What sets you apart is following the story. You are a remarkable journalist rather than a tourist. And the story may continue over a few days or even months. Recognising the full story gives you entry to the process, thinking, learning, encounter, exploration, product, value, resonance or transference you've captured.

The same photo, or sequence of photos, can be used for many alternate functions. They could be used to discuss at a staff meeting. They assist in communication in a parent interview. If you have family meetings with the children present, photos can be offered to the students so they can verbalise what they've been doing, what they value and what they have learned. Repurposing data is a lifesaver. The photographs, like the conversations, are what capture the pathway of children's learning.

Products

Capture, curate, communicate.

Products are the way your assessment is displayed or communicated. Flexible primary data can be quickly accessed and customised into different products. If it's for your own planning, you can have it static on your desktop to review when you need it. If it's to prompt discussion with your colleagues, make a quick PowerPoint presentation. Select and print what you need for a parent reflection book outside the room. Load a photo montage on a digital photo frame. Add it to the collection of documentation you are organising to show the authorities who may drop in unexpectedly or by appointment to assess your centre.

What you capture is evidence of your good practice. Send a short description and photo to a specialist working with a child on an issue. Report on the children's progress with them or with their parents. Share at conferences, in network meetings and the broader community the great work you are doing. Create documentation panels for your classroom, which interpret and communicate the learning in your program. Plan a school or public exhibition. The same primary data can be reorganised, reinterpreted, curated and presented to accomplish whatever you need. You can copy, paste and customise it because you know the deep meaning and value of what you have captured.

Privacy

Private assessments are shared with parents or possibly specialist clinicians working with individual children. They are protected by privacy legislation and are not to be shared with any other parties. This record of a child's personal progress in all domains is usually shared in interviews with parents and your semester and year-end reports.

Publicity

The children's curricular progress and play experiences are often presented in a reflection journal or book for parents to view. This is public data, and care needs to be taken to ensure that it is fair to all concerned. It is a vehicle for educators to demonstrate the learning journey of children and to make their thinking visible. When it's public, make sure all children are in the reflections at some stage. If parents know that your mini projects are run in small groups, and not all the children are interested in some of them, they'll accept that. But they will expect you to include their child in another mini project sometime in the year. Also, be completely aware of the filters we spoke about earlier related to culture, gender and other considerations.

In summary

Regarding assessment, we consider the eight Ps:
1. Purpose
2. Processes
3. Practicality
4. Progress
5. Primary and secondary sources
6. Products
7. Privacy
8. Publicity

Chapter 7
In words we meet the world
Harnessing the structure of language

> *Consciousness is reflected in the word like the sun is reflected in a droplet of water. The word is a microcosm of consciousness, related to consciousness like a living cell is related to an organism, like an atom is related to the cosmos. The meaningful word is a microcosm of human consciousness.*
> Lev Vygotsky (Rieber, Carton, & (eds), 1987, p. 285)

In this chapter, I talk about language in many different ways. I offer trends, structures and strategies that you can use whenever you are among children to scaffold their language knowledge and conceptual understanding. Discussing language in detail is essential, as we realise that playing alone is not enough. Through building vocabulary, comprehension and structures, teachers or primary carers can scaffold children's concepts early and help them organise their reasoning and thinking into valuable structures.

Top-level structures

A few times now, I have shared moments where a new insight has changed how I think. One such transformation occurred during a presentation by Brendan Bartlett (Bartlett, 2003) at a Mind Brain conference in Melbourne.

He lectured on Top-Level Structures of language. The gist is that if you understand the structure, you are more likely to understand the content. This is so common sense it beggars belief that I found it so illuminating.

But it's true of everything. If you can't see the structure, you have a limited grasp of it. It is just a cog in something, and you don't know what that something is.

The AHA moment took what I knew about language structures and applied it to how I could mobilise it every minute of every day when I was in contact with children.

The lack of time is the most common cause of being overwhelmed in any educational setting. We don't have enough! I often hear: 'I'd love to include x in my curriculum, but it is crammed to capacity and overflowing'.

This chapter is about magnifying literacy without adding one second to your schedule. And that was what excited me about what Bartlett had said. I was a walking, talking literacy machine. Every time I opened my mouth, I had the possibility of supporting children's construction of language.

Also, the literacy artefacts I brought into the room to resource the program gained a more profound significance. Every picture book I read represented every picture book the children would encounter in the future. The same goes for every letter, poem, chapter book and drama piece. I had a code to share with them. We could unpack and interpret any literary structure we shared at their current level of engagement.

When we discuss the seven learning zones in the following few chapters, the importance of language development is a constant motif because concepts are built on language comprehension.

In narrative or writing, there is the ubiquitous structure of beginning, middle and end. Or there is a juxtaposition between two things being compared. Problem and solution and cause and effect are recognisable structures. Even the humble list is a language structure.

The most excellent literature builds suspense because it breaks these structures. It messes with our predictions of what is next. A great novel makes you work hard to build up a picture by drip-feeding your information. You make one logical connection at a time. The puzzle starts to unfold about a character's true persona or the significance of events on a particular day. Logical relationships are embedded across the whole story. Structure is the coherence of things in logical relationships. In the novel, we are made to work seriously hard to solve the mysteries – and we love it! The novel's author injects dramatic irony and suspense, and we who enjoy the book know the rules.

Even the list is not random. There is not much in common between milk and a toothbrush unless they are on your shopping list. Then you identify the relationship.

In one instance, Bartlett worked with children who were not natural or motivated writers. All he offered them was a list. Tell me about snakes. So, they listed ten different things about them. Once the list was on the page, the ideas were sorted according to different logical connections.

The snake was an egg first and grew later. It lived in a burrow. It was patterned a certain way for its own protection and camouflage; people feared it, but it was of great cultural importance. From kids who were opposed to writing, they created a fluid, logically connected, interesting and meaningful story. They had a key. Within the story, they surfaced concepts of time, location, function, significance, perspective and culture. All this from a list!

When we open our mouths, we can share these structures with children. Whether in preschool or early primary school, we can magically build language.

But we're ahead of ourselves; we've started at the top level!

The literacy iceberg

Presenters Dr Avis Ridgeway (Monash University) and Chris Celada, then Senior Lecturer (Holmesglen TAFE), spoke about early literacy at a teachers' network meeting a few years ago. They used the image of an iceberg. The very tip of the iceberg is reading and writing. These highly complex skills are built on an inordinate number of foundational skills.

A child must have developed a conceptual understanding of spatial relationships to accurately write a single letter of the alphabet onto a page. What is top, bottom, sideways, left, right, middle, curvy, straight, round, long, short, upside down and right way up. Students must coordinate a perceptual motor plan in their mind before activating the muscular, fine-motor control to create the letter 'a'. Besides this, there is the comprehension that the 'a' is a symbolic representation of a sound made by the voice, that it is part of a word that is part of a sentence…

Then, beyond writing letters, students must understand the meaning of the words, the meaning of different kinds of sentences and how all the elements are used to formulate communicative products.

Composition of the literacy iceberg

Literacy is hugely important.

It is another great cause of debate in the early years. When do we teach the alphabet, phonics or early reading, and how do we teach it? Tons of papers have been written addressing these dilemmas.

There is no definitive answer.

Some children are reading by three years of age, while others only get there when they are five, six or even seven. Usually, they are all reading and writing by eight years of age. In Scandinavia, they don't start with reading and writing until later, and in the UK, children start at four.

But you shouldn't throw up your arms because there is no precise answer. There are a multitude of things you *can do* as you work with children throughout the day so that whenever they can read or work towards their pen licence, they have the knowledge and familiarity with language structures to make their efforts fluid and meaningful.

In her book *Thirty Million Words*, Dana Suskind mentions we can 'tune in' to what children say, and 'talk more' to scaffold their language learning (Suskind, 2015).

Tune in

Leveraging experiential schemas

We already know that children's first understanding is experiential, and in the discussion on foundational knowledge, I explained schema theory, the laying down of sensory memories.

Why is it important to know about schema theory?

Knowing the power of sensory learning gives us a deeper understanding of what might be happening in the minds of pre-verbal children. We see greater significance in their actions and behaviours.

In older children we can harness this sensory pathway to understanding by offering children metaphors to explain complex ideas. My sister is a maths teacher and often suggests a sensory memory for children to imagine complex ideas. When they don't know what concentric is, she might say: imagine a dart board. She suggests the crystals in a chandelier for an expanding and rising pattern. The knowledge and memory of concrete sensory experience is a powerful vehicle for learning in older students, and it is equally based on schema theory.

I watched a two-year-old child conduct an experiment entirely of her own devising. There were tall, long-leaved plants in the playground, and the leaves were attached to a woody stalk. The plants were double her height. She had hold of the stalk and was gently shaking the leaves at the top and making a sound like: 'hurrr, hurrr, hurrr, for each shake.

Suddenly, she stopped and looked around. About five metres away, there was another plant the same. She gave her plant a few more shakes, then went to the other plant, took the stalk and mirrored precisely what she had just been doing.

She had ignored every other tree, plant and shrub in the yard. She had found one that was exactly the same and anticipated that it would behave the same in her hands. This is remarkable.

When we notice it, we can interpret the processes of comparison, evaluation, prediction and hypothetical thinking she employed. And we are in a position to offer her the language that accompanies what she has been doing. 'Goodness, Ella, you noticed that those plants are exactly the same and they are not even next to each other.'

In a room of three-year-olds, children were given some of those fabulous decorating cards adults use when they are researching the colour for their perfect feature wall. They were all shades of green, and leaves of different colours were displayed to match the cards. It was a great investigation table.

On a comfortable couch across the room, a child was reading a book on her own. She put the book down beside her and took off. I thought she'd lost interest. No, she went to the investigation table, took three or four of the cards, returned to her book and tried to match the green colours of images in the book.

Again, this is hypothetical thinking, transferring experiences across space.

If we know there is experimentation in their actions, we can support children's understanding and expression of their exploration and conclusions with greater clarity.

Shared gaze

During tuning in, the adult respects the child's focus. It is engagement with what the student is doing. Children are open to hearing about what they are attending to. (I think this works with everyone, really.) Young students experiencing this begin to see themselves as having a respected role in a social dialogue.

An example of how to leverage schemas could be toddlers and three-year-olds carrying buckets of water over a short distance and pouring the liquid into the sandpit. They are 'understanding' what they are doing via many sensations. The way the water behaves as it moves becomes apparent to them. They feel the qualities of the water: weight, volume, flow, spills or qualities of the sand: absorption, texture, porousness, etc. As they repeat the activity, they adjust their balance, develop a sense of expectation and engage in prediction. Although experiential learning is language-free, *it can be enhanced by connecting it to language.*

When the child returns after a few trips, we can remark that they are balancing the bucket better, spilling less water and getting better at the task. We can ask what they expect to see… and, if they have the language, let them answer or answer the question for them.

'What is happening to the water? Is it sinking into the sand? Does it happen every time?' Then comment: 'You know what to expect now, don't you? You've seen it happen a few times!'

They may not fully understand all the commentary, but they will get the gist and understand that what they are doing is clearly of interest and value. This will make them more self-conscious of the task and begin to develop functional receptive language in the context around the activity.

Providing language within the context of the young student's activity and exploration is more effective than delivering decontextualised language.

Expand the goals of your communication

> 'Language is a process of free creation; its laws and principles are fixed, but the manner in which the principles of generation are used is free and infinitely varied. Even the interpretation and use of words involves a process of free creation.' (Noam Chomsky)

We can provide language for specific reasons.

Your comment or question can relate to the emotional aspect of the task, or to the cognitive component. You refer to how carefully the task is being done, that the young person must be proud of their activity, that it has meaning to others, etc.

Some informational comments might be: 'You have the bright red bucket with the white handle, I think this is the fourth time you have completed this circuit. Four times there and four times back! A lot of fun as you work hard!' Did you use your own bucket when you were on holiday at the beach with Mum and Dad?'

When this conversation occurs around the activity, the child is learning how words occur in language frames. They construct elements of language by responding to repeated patterns. They can now connect the experience to the world outside of the self. They meet the world in words.

Talk more

Magnify the impact of your words

In our daily communications we can be aware of the language structures we are sharing.

We can say, 'I'm going to ask you a *question*. Which area would you like to go and play in now?' And we can respond when they tell us, 'Thank you for your *answer*. Off you go then.'

Similarly: 'I am about to tell you all something', 'give you a list of instructions' or 'tell you a story.'

Another way your minute-by-minute speech can scaffold literacy is to be specific and say, 'Please pick up that book and put it on the shelf. The place feels really organised when things are where they belong, don't you think?'

Your longer response provides the labels for more than one item and explains the action without taking up much more time.

What is going on in our minds and our reasons for saying and doing things is generally invisible to children, so talking out loud gives them entry into our thinking processes and access to our logical connections. It helps children when we vocalise our thinking. Not only do they learn words for things in context, but they also learn about your cognitive processes. They also learn about temporal and spatial relationships.

Thinking aloud is often called soliloquy, and children who listen to what we think are more able to make connections. When we talk aloud, children develop a theory of mind over time. They understand that others have thoughts and that those thoughts might be different from their own.

When you talk about something, it helps to **connect it to the more general category** it comes from. Rather than say, 'That is blue', you might say, 'That is a blue *colour*', or 'That is a square, triangular, round *shape*'. 'Would you like the big *size* or the small *size*?'

Another valuable hack is **adding process words** for cognition. 'I was *planning* for us to go outdoors now, but I *noticed* it is raining. I had to *reconsider* and *change my mind*. I *think* it will be better if we eat our lunch first and *make a new plan* later. Who agrees with me?' You elaborate instead of either simply changing the plan without saying anything at all, or saying, 'It's raining, so we'll eat now and go out later.'

By **adding cognitive load**, we can extend children's short-term memory and comprehension. Begin with one instruction and then add one more at a time, ensuring they successfully carry them out. When you frame the instructions, include conceptual information:

'Please put your Lego building where we usually do on the shelf outside to the right of the door.'

'Collect your hat and your lunch from your locker, then cross the foyer and sit down outside on the top step near teacher Jane.'

Finally, now that you have the reasoning, you can add many examples of your own and get children to use similes.

'This shape reminds me of something. What do you think it is like?' Children might say, 'It looks like the letter L' or 'It looks like a ring.'

This sets children up to understand the use of similes and metaphors, which is essential for **understanding figurative and inferential language**. When discussing friendship, caring or any topic, you might ask, 'What colour do you think friendship is?', Or 'What's the best shape for friendship?' 'What is the sound of friendship?'

The last part of this conversation has **open-ended questions**. This is a key to developing independent and creative thinking. Mainly use 'why' questions rather than 'what' questions. Once children have learned from your soliloquised thinking out loud, these open-ended questions encourage them to think for themselves and provide their own reasons.

> 'A child who is encouraged to think creatively when very young will likely have a stronger foundation for learning at the beginning of school. Creativity is not talent or skill; rather it is the tendency toward exploration, discovery and imagination' (Suskind, 2015, p. 150).

As Dana Suskind in her book *Thirty Million Words* explains, it's not the quantity but the quality of the words that counts (Suskind, 2015).

Discussing language in such detail is important because we realise that play alone is not enough. Through the mediation of educators, be they parents or teachers, students can be scaffolded early to organise their reasoning and thinking into valuable structures.

They lay down the wiring not only for understanding the here and now, but also for transcending the moment and building the neural pathways that habituate the connection of ideas. Connection is crucial, and the pathways for it have to be actively developed.

This knowledge enables us to enhance our own and students' understanding at every moment of every day in the early years environment. We can use these moments, or they can pass us by.

I have spoken about precision and structure. And below is a wonderful quote about that:

> 'A man with a scant vocabulary will almost certainly be a weak thinker. The richer and more copious one's vocabulary and the greater one's awareness of fine distinctions and subtle nuances of meaning, the more fertile and precise is likely to be one's thinking. Knowledge of things and knowledge of the words for them grow together. If you do not know the words, you can hardly know the thing' (Henry Hazlitt, *Thinking as a Science*, 1916).

Of course, human beings and the world are so marvellous and infinite that, in some ways, even the most precise language cannot adequately describe their beauty and complexity!

> 'The struggle of literature is in fact a struggle to escape from the confines of language; it stretches out from the utmost limits of what can be said; what stirs literature is the call and attraction of what is not in the dictionary' (Italo Calvino).

13 key relationships that organise information

Below are 13 key relationships revealed in structured language. I have found this list of questions indispensable when teaching because it prompts me to consider precisely which concept and relationship I wish students to focus and expand on.

1. **Qualifying:** What is it?
2. **Analytical:** How can it be analysed into whole and parts?
3. **Functional:** How does it work? What makes it work?
4. **Temporal relationship:** How is it placed or related in time?
5. **Spatial relationship:** How is it placed or related in space?
6. **Comparative relationship:** How is it equivalent, similar or different?
7. **Causal relationship:** What is the cause and effect?
8. **Dependence:** What is dependent on something, and what is independent?
9. **Transformational:** What has changed; how and why?
10. **Quantifying:** How can it be measured?
11. **Hypothetical:** If this happens, what might follow?
12. **Ethical:** What is our responsibility in relation to it?
13. **Imaginative:** How might it be?

In summary

- Language has top-level structures that give it logical integrity. Lists, cause–effect and problem–solution relationships, comparative juxtaposition and chronological sequences are examples
- Language builds through several levels: from experiential schemas, through labelling, to combining words in phrases and sentences. Sentences combine within more complex goal-oriented formats
- Knowing the structures enhances rather than impedes creativity
- Language is the bridge between the here and now and the abstract realm in which we both encode and decode our understanding of the world
- Language is the way we understand ourselves and others
- Language is how we learn about how we learn
- Language is how we transfer knowledge across contexts
- According to Loris Malaguzzi, languages are expressive, communicative, symbolic, cognitive, ethical, metaphorical, logical, imaginative and relational (Cagliari et al., 2016)

PART C

THE AGILITY WHEEL

SEVEN DYNAMIC PLAY AND LEARNING ZONES

Chapter 8
The agility wheel

Agility within and of itself is a strategy.
Pearl Zhu

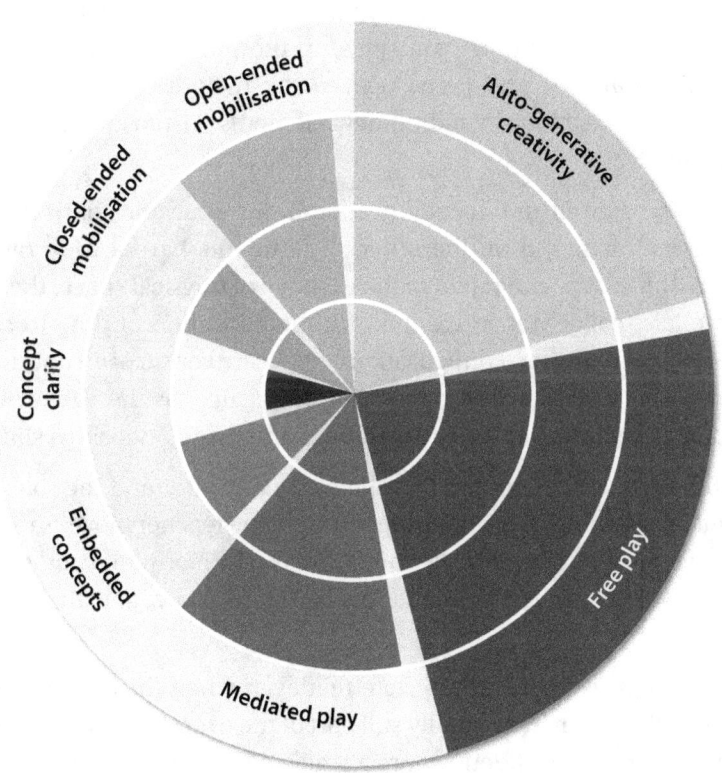

Figure 13: The agility wheel

Agility: the quality or state of being agile – nimbleness, dexterity.

The ability to think and understand quickly

Agile is a state of mind (Zhu, 2016). Pearl Zhu describes agility as people-centric, empathetic and focused on improvement. It is not about totally free thinking, but taking account of structure, having discipline and deploying the right skills at the right time.

You spend time resourcing your learning spaces with materials, planning activities and experiences, taking students on excursions, and organising incursions. All of this is to create a rich and varied platform for learning. Within this planning and resourcing I am sure you are conscious of wanting to honour the agency of your students at the same time as your curriculum goals are being met.

I've described you as a choreographer; now, see yourself as a conductor.

You can conduct a concerto, where all the elements are known, practised and performed perfectly. And sometimes, that is precisely what you want to do. But at another time, you spice up the program with jazz, where the rhythms are set and perhaps even the melody. Still, the script is open to improvisation, including new elements, virtuoso performances and creativity.

On the one side of the agency spectrum, an educator controls highly scripted learning, and on the other, the students have a wide range of choices. The choice can relate to the expanse of physical space, the range of materials, collaborative grouping or the allocation of time to a task. There are many other configurations between very close scripting for students and students' free range. But in essence, as the agency of the educator and student shifts, the dynamics and the relationships shift.

The shift involves changes in the role of the educator and the role of the student. As learning becomes more scripted, the teacher moves in and the range of choice narrows, the learning goal is predetermined and specific. When creativity is the focus, the teacher steps away, and the range of choice widens.

At this stage, it is important to state that even when the students' range increases, their activity is usually still part of the overall curriculum vision. Learning zones give students more agency in how the projected learning is encountered and acquired.

Sometimes, student-initiated investigations or projects are given great value and included in the plan. However, when discussing creativity, we do not randomly follow multiple paths. There is intellectual rigour, not randomness, behind the use of the zones – intellectual rigour that values both conventional close-ended vertical learning and the creative use of conceptual learning towards open-ended destinations.

In Part C of this book, I invite you to engage with seven learning zones, each with distinctive form and character. The rationale for doing this is so that you can shift zones and deploy each with the same fluency you use when driving your car. You can change gears, directions, speed and destination to optimise students' learning.

In any learning zone, there is a three-way relationship between the educator, the student and the task. The word 'task' here is not the traditional definition of a task set by a teacher, but rather what is currently being attended to in the brain. The task is the current cognition. So, using a rake to gather leaves in the playground and jumping in to enjoy the crunching sensation is a task.

When we teach directly, there is a close connection between the educator and the task. The educator has more control over the task, and the student is the receiver of information and instructions.

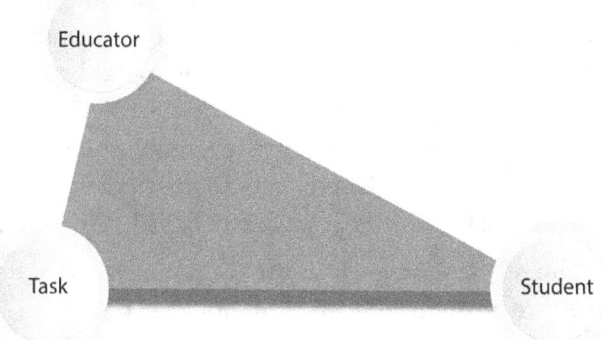

Figure 14: Educational configuration 1

If the student's agency is magnified, then the zone will change. The task will move away from the educator, and the student's range of choice will open up.

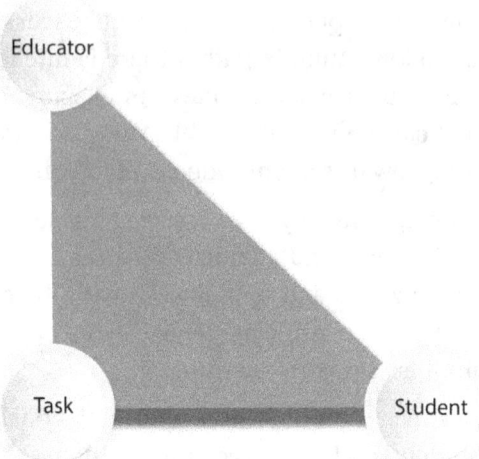

Figure 15: Educational configuration 2

In addition to change in agency, the education can be one-tiered or two-tiered. The learning can be content-based or include awareness of thinking processes. Understanding the processes and relationships within and across content makes the knowledge more transferable. You can teach concepts or amplify the effect and teach for conceptual understanding.

For this book, I have selected seven characteristic learning zones and represented them on an 'agility wheel' (see page 97). The wheel has four concentric circles, each at intervals of one unit in measurement from the centre. And I have distributed seven zone maps within the 360° area. I have left 5° between each zone to emphasise that they *are independent* of one another. Each zone is defined by two measures: a linear distance representing the proximity of the educator to the student and an angle in degrees, representing the range of choice available to the student.

Starting at a unit of 1 is strategic because we can never be at 0 proximity. At no stage can we be in the child's mind. But level one is the closest and most directive we can be. So, for example, in free play, the teacher is four units away, and the child has 85° of choice (4:85°).

Seven learning zones

1. Free play (4:85°)
2. Mediated play (3:50°)

3. Embedded concepts (2:30°)
4. Concept clarity (1:25°)
5. Closed-ended mobilisation (2:25°)
6. Open-ended mobilisation (3:35°)
7. Auto-generative creativity (4:75°)

As mentioned above, range can refer to physical range, where children have more geographic freedom, as in free play; but it mainly relates to the intentional landscape. What are the goals of each of the participants in each zone?

Clearly, other educators may like to expand or reduce the range or distance of a zone or even add other characteristic zones, but the general idea of the relationship between proximity and range of choice will prevail. The zones I have defined here have been formulated during decades of working with students of all ages. They are common learning configurations in educational contexts, particularly in early years environments.

The learning zones are not learning stages. Each one is independent of the others, has different goals and allows the educator to maintain an agile stance.

It is important to emphasise that the size of the segment in the agility wheel does not relate to its importance or the time it should take up in a curriculum plan. *Every zone is equally valuable.*

The projected use of the wheel is that teachers can easily distinguish the zones. They can balance their curriculum by planning for and resourcing based on the relationships in each zone. They will be able to recognise the opportunities to pivot from one zone to another to leverage a current incident, action or idea. They will have the awareness to use what is happening in one zone to further a goal in another. In short, it is vital to have the agility to know where and when to animate any one of the zones. This could be done during planning or in the current process. Educators conduct the flow of their own and their students' agency.

In the seven chapters that follow, each learning zone will be defined and discussed in terms of its distinctive elements. Each chapter outlines the educator's role and the student's role in the focus zone. The chapter for each zone suggests relevant resources and ideas for scaffolding concept learning and offers categories of assessment and means of evidence collection.

In summary

- The agility wheel represents seven distinctive learning zones
- Within these zones, the agency of the teacher and the child changes; in some, the student has more freedom to follow their own goals, and in others, the range closes and the activities are more scripted by the educator
- Each zone is given two measures related to the teacher's proximity or distance from the student; the second refers to the students' range of freedom to select their goals and activities
- The distance is in units 1–4, and the range is measured in degrees
- The zones are independent of each other, not stages in a learning cycle
- The size of the segment for each zone does not represent importance or time spent in that zone; it is about the different interactions, roles and goals of the student and educator
- No segment has a specific relationship to the segments adjacent to them
- The educator may plan a zone and deploy it for curriculum purposes, but he or she may pivot into another zone to optimise a current, incidental situation
- The ranges selected are based on the author's experience over decades of teaching at different year levels, including a lengthy time in early years education (how long will not be disclosed!)

Chapter 9
Free play

The playing adult steps sideward into another reality; the playing child advances forward to new stages of mastery.
Erik H Erikson

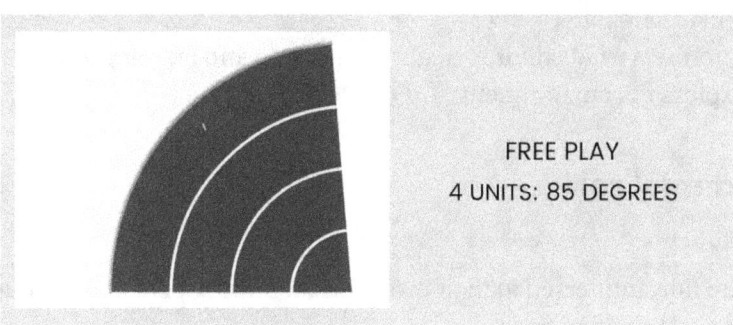

Figure 16: Free play

Coordinates

Students' free play occurs at the maximum distance of four units from the educator on the agility wheel. Students have the widest range of choice at 85° (4:85°).

Definition

Free play is an outdoor or indoor learning zone where children follow their lead. They select the equipment, materials, location and playing partners to suit the activity of their devising. They formulate their own goals and are often in a state of flow. It is the least scripted learning zone. Whatever they are learning is self-initiated.

Educator's role

The educator:
- Selects and provides a broad array of equipment and materials for children to use independently. Some standard materials are always available, and for novelty and variety, others are introduced for short periods of time
- Provides materials and equipment to support the enhancement of physical and cognitive skills
- Considers equipment to encourage individual and collaborative play
- May be invited into a closer range by children who wish to engage with the adult
- Observes and assesses social and emotional patterns of behaviour and wellbeing
- Interprets what children might be thinking and learning as they explore the environment

Students' role

The students:
- Are fully immersed in their own world following personal intentions at a self-defined pace
- Exercise independence and select from an array of equipment and materials
- Choose their own play companions
- Practise and consolidate social and communication skills
- Internalise the qualities of materials and how they transform in relation to different influences in the environment
- Develop language competence, sense of self and theory of mind in the company of their peers

About free play

Seriously, a chapter in a book cannot for one second capture the meaning and value of play! You know it and I know it. There are excellent books on play-based learning with an enormous body of evidence about its importance for learning (Walker & Bass, 2015), (Singer et al., 2006).

There are several well-documented kinds of play. Children engage in individual play, parallel play, interactive play, fantasy play, tabletop play, physical movement and games, digital, virtual and other kinds. The play is good for social and emotional wellbeing and education as well as cognitive education. The range of resources for children is endless.

Sensory learning, as discussed in detail earlier is extremely relevant during free play. You will remember the examples of children carrying water, shaking plants and other means of understanding the world through their senses. Because of your awareness of this pathway to learning, I am sure that as you observe play, you will be attuned to sensory learning and interpret what might be going on in children's thinking as they manipulate and use materials and interact with one another.

Your assessment when children are at play is generally done at a distance. In the preschool, no play goes unsupervised. So, you are in a situation where we can map and observe patterns in children's play without scripting it or getting involved. You notice whether children are constant loners. If solo play is out of character for their peers, you can consider the reasons; and if you need to do something to change the current situation, you can plan it. If children always have the same group of friends, you ask yourself, is it worthwhile implementing strategies to introduce some flexibility? Are children only using one or two areas and not being very adventurous?

At one of the schools I consulted, the educators mapped the geography of children's play in the outdoor area daily. Over time, they noticed that children gravitated to naturally vegetated, more private and shadier areas. They also noticed which materials and equipment were more popular, which caused the most conflict and which introduced harmonious play. They entirely took on board the idea of listening to the children and respecting the image of the child (Rinaldi, 2001). They used the free play zone as an opportunity for research to elevate their practice.

When children are in unscripted play, it doesn't mean that they won't seek out the educators. But they choose the distance. If you want them to engage with you, you must be approachable and open. More scripted activities can develop from free play when children share their thoughts. I discussed earlier the wings project, which started this way.

Figure 17: Child absorbed in play

Figure 18: Free water play in group

If there are difficulties or conflicts, they will generally surface. When you deal with these situations, in effect, you have shifted zones. You move closer to listen, to arbitrate and educate for fairer or more harmonious outcomes.

Free play is also where you can observe the development of children's gross- and/or fine-motor coordination. When working with a child who was left behind in the pre-skills for reading and writing in Prep, it was clear that many of the milestones for gross-motor and fine-motor skills were unpractised and unconsolidated. Right- and left-handedness, crossing the midline, perceptual motor planning and coordination are critical for reading and writing. You can keep checklists and observe children or have a fun event where everyone hops, skips, jumps and gallops across the basketball court one day so you can ensure everyone is progressing well.

Over time, you check that they can roll, balance, run, hop, skip, gallop, jump on one and both legs, slide, climb, hang and alternate movements fluently. You can also check gait, stance, posture and rhythm. Gross-motor development precedes fine-motor development, and so during free art activities and tabletop play, these skills can also be observed: pinch, clasp, lift, cut, paste, carry objects, arrange materials, hold and use painting, drawing and writing implements, roll (e.g. plasticine and clay), stack objects and balance objects.

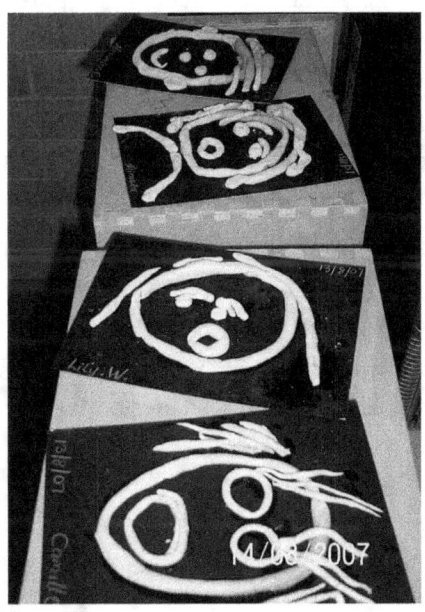

Figure 19: Rolling and pinching techniques for clay

I think it is important to attune the early primary educators among you to the cognitive and conceptual, rather than the wellbeing and emotional, advantages which can be gained through play. Many of you already know its value. However, curriculum demands, or parent expectations, often drive play out at the primary level. Independent play can be the basis of great learning and creativity. This is especially true for literacy and mathematics education.

In several of the schools where I have consulted, primary teachers were sceptical about the curricular value of play. But they were prepared to experiment and timetable a play session every morning for about 20 minutes. They immediately knew how it revealed students' knowledge, interests and motivation to learn.

When the group assembled for the day, the children, on their own or with their play companions, communicated to the class what they had been doing. The teachers were staggered by the complex interrelationships within the play, the quality of the use of materials and how the play was often infused with what children were learning in other curriculum areas. Children from Foundation though Year 2 were documenting and elaborating their ideas and products using voice recording, photography and other applications. When the teachers compared standard literacy and maths statistics with those of students in prior years, they were amazed at the overall increase in the measures for both maths and literacy skills.

Children's play is highly complex. It displays principles of order, use of prior knowledge, creativity, hierarchical relationships, communication, negotiation and total engagement.

Free access to construction, art, literacy or science-based activity engages the senses, the mind and the emotions to cohere in the formulation of skills and understanding.

During free play, your role is that of an observer, assessor and researcher rather than an active participant in learning goals.

In summary

- During free play, the educator is at a unit of four in distance and the students have the widest range of choice at 85° (4:85°)
- Free play is extremely important in early years settings
- Its relevance and value in emotional, social and cognitive development is well documented

- When assessing play, we gain from mapping the way children interact with others
- We can plan to improve children's social and emotional wellbeing by being alert to the patterns of their emotional tone and integration
- It is valuable to map both children's negotiation of play, including where they spend most their time and what they are employing in their play
- There are endless resources for play, and it is an activity that motivates children to discover and explore
- Play is as important in primary settings as in preschool settings, but children engage with concepts at a more complex and abstract level
- Students are at liberty to approach educators during unscripted play, so it is worthwhile to remain open to their willingness to engage
- From free engagements with educators, new projects might ensue, or children's thoughts can be included in the learning flow elsewhere in the program

Chapter 10
Mediated play

...to understand something is to assimilate it into an appropriate schema.
Richard Skemp

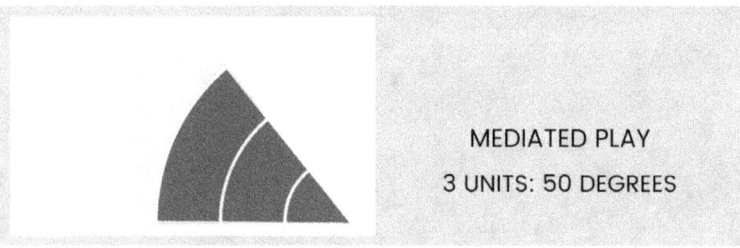

Figure 20: Mediated play

Coordinates

During mediated play, the educator is proximally closer than free play at a distance of three units. The students' range of choice is narrower but still reasonably extensive at 50° (3:50°).

Definition

Mediated play is an outdoor or indoor learning zone where the educator steps into students' play to promote concept learning. The equipment provided is more restricted than in free play. It is selected for its potential to demonstrate learning concepts. Students still develop their own goals and intentions. The teacher enters the play not to direct it but to extend it in the direction of the student's own goals. The educator provides vocabulary, introduces concepts or offers explanations relative to what the children are doing. The students' play is unscripted, but the educator's mediation is intentional and purposeful. The goal of mediated play is to enrich the child's play with relevant contextual information about their activity and thinking processes. Mediated play is a version of shared gaze, where the educator joins in with what the children are already doing. The educator identifies opportunities to assess receptive language, enhance vocabulary and expressive language, improve skills and broaden conceptual and relational understanding using scaffolding techniques. They also listen for ways to extend ideas children have imagined or created as a prompt for further learning.

During mediated play, the educator helps students' growing conceptual understanding of various concepts over time. There is no immediate time frame for complete comprehension.

Educator's role

The educator:

- Selects and provides an array of equipment and materials for children to use by themselves. The materials are chosen for their potential to demonstrate concepts
- Respects the goals and current activity of the students and 'shares their gaze'
- Assesses the students' current understanding of selected concepts
- Purposefully and intentionally steps into children's play as a mediator to enhance and progress conceptual knowledge and understanding in the direction of the student's intentions
- Observes and assesses what children are doing to provide new vocabulary, bring awareness to concepts and provide explanations if required
- Considers the next level up in students' conceptual understanding
- May suggest extensions for the play

Students' role

The students:

- Are fully immersed in their own play, following personal intentions at their own pace

- Display independence and select from the available materials and equipment
- Choose their play companions
- Practise and combine social and communication skills
- Learn the qualities of materials and how they transform due to different influences in the environment
- Are alerted by the educator to new language and concepts related to their activity
- Develop language, concepts and significance of what they are doing in relation to learning new things

About mediated play

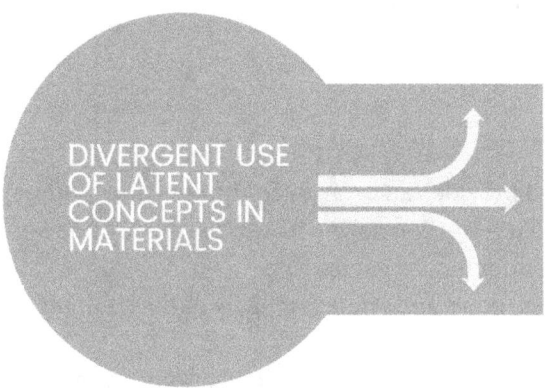

Figure 21: Divergent use of latent concepts

In mediated play, you offer a narrower selection of resources than in free play. While you are aware of the potential of the materials to demonstrate several concepts, *you are not particular about which concepts are activated during mediated play*. The mediational scaffolding is done around students' own intentions. You are focusing on where the child's interests lie and expand thinking from there. You choose the one or two directly relevant to the current play from the many underlying concepts.

A block has weight, height, width, volume, etc. The idea of mediational scaffolding is not to emphasise all of them. You tune in to what the child is doing with the block – and reveal the relevant concept. The child might not need information about the block's dimensions because it is used as a telephone! The ideas that emerge then are around formats of communication. The child has invested the block with an idiosyncratic meaning and you enter the play respecting that.

Figure 22: Big block play

As the child talks into the block, you ask: 'Who are you ringing? Did they say hello back? What is the message? Are you making an appointment?' The object represents the format of a conversation, with its purpose and reciprocal structure. Talking on the telephone relies on vocal communication without the additional codes of gesture or facial expression. (Unless, of course, the kid is pretending to be on FaceTime!)

Experiential learning versus mediated learning during play

When a student encounters and uses materials, there is experiential learning. The materials give direct feedback. The learning may include language, but it might also only be in the domain of sensory or perceptual motor understanding. I've often stressed that this is not to be underestimated. Sensory intelligence tunes our sense of body position so we successfully move and position ourselves and objects in space. It is also vital for motor planning, a sub-skill in writing and many other educational tasks. It is only when you work with a child who does not demonstrate automatic perceptual motor alertness, that you realise how important it is.

Perception is not only related to the physical world. For instance, it is a motor perceptual skill to mentally connect two dots with a line before you draw the line. Without the perceptual plan, the physical attempt might fail.

Your goal during guided learning is to move children beyond direct sensory or motor learning to enhance and progress conceptual and relational understanding.

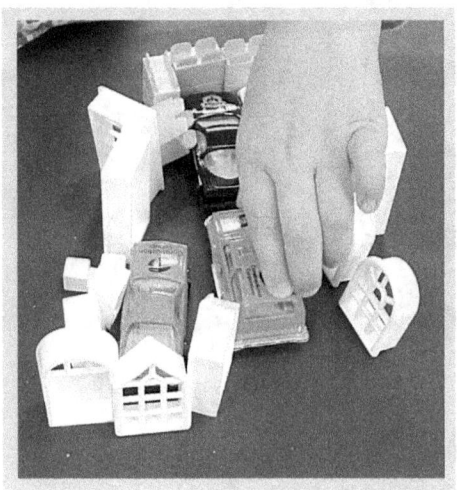

Figure 23: A child sensing enclosed space

The idea is to link children's current activity and exploration to current knowledge. You want them to identify their explorations with new nouns and verbs. They should use vocabulary to explain relationships that enable the learning in new contexts. Examples of the kinds of concepts you can highlight are: colour, form and shape, size, number, measurement, orientation in space, similarity, difference, equivalence, function, texture, time, sequence, order, arrangement, grouping, change, causation, pattern, symmetry.

Figure 24: Comparison and measurement

You don't use all these words, only what is appropriate. When children carry something heavy, you can ask them if it is more or less heavy than something else. (Comparison.) You can ask them why they think it is very heavy. (Causation.) Ask them to explain where objects are in space, like what is at the very top, the first, last or middle thing. (Location.)

When kids line something up by colour, you can talk about matching, sorting or grouping. When they use material to build a dinosaur lair or a bird's nest, you can alert them or extend their knowledge to habitats or life cycles.

You watch what they are doing and inquire into their actions or the stories they are telling. Their actions and descriptions reveal their knowledge levels, interests and progress in their thinking over time. This is an active assessment.

Clearly, what occurs in supportive interactions can be used to further curriculum goals. The pauses and conversations can be brought to the whole group's attention. Children can explain their ideas and discoveries, and the *ownership is credited to them*.

Collecting evidence

Besides the cognitive goals, this is also an opportunity to observe children's perseverance, frustration levels, blocking, cooperation, collaboration and other dispositional and affective aspects that affect learning.

Evidence of learning is collected using photography or video, recording brief conversations, taking quick observations and using lists to tick off on consolidated skills. As discussed in an earlier chapter on assessment, be aware of capturing the whole story. Sometimes this emerges over a few days or weeks rather than in a single play session.

The assessment can be done for early maths, literacy, fine-motor skills, construction, logical reasoning, planning, an extension of previous efforts and many other areas.

For early maths, you might be assessing the numbers, sorting, shape recognition, patterning, symmetry, spatial awareness, one-to-one correspondence and base ten concepts.

Scaffolding and extension

A mediational intervention is often the small prompt a child needs to connect with their own motivation and open new vistas of knowledge.

Drawing is a good example. Some children can look at an object, work out the key features and set to work drawing it. Say it is an elephant. The drawing may be a curly line and an enclosed shape, but the information has been transferred.

Other children find it difficult to separate the individual elements from the whole. They benefit from being asked mediational questions like: 'What is this animal? What parts do you see? Which is the front, and which is the back? How many legs does it have? Is the tail thick or thin? What shape is the body, head, ears, etc? Which part would you like to draw first?'

During these mediational questions, the student's attention is directed to how the whole and parts are related and to the features of each part.

When the child has gone through the different parts, they are more likely to see how to adjust the elephant in the drawing. Once the process is repeated a few times, they carry it over to other situations. A student who joined my K4 group late in the year lacked drawing confidence. I asked her to draw a butterfly and offered two shapes: an oval for the wings and a triangle for the body. With this simple prompt, she moved from being completely blocked to being one of the most skilled drawers in the group. It switched her brain on to the technique. Suddenly, she could see to draw.

A second example of unlocking awareness is a child who was dependent on a particular play partner, his cousin, and his play area, Lego building. His choices were Lego build with his cousin or Lego build on your own.

On one occasion, he and his cousin had been away for a camping weekend. I asked them to draw their experience together to shift the dependent child's range of abilities. When they brought it over after a while, I suggested they take some blue paper to represent the ocean. They enthusiastically went to the paper shelf for the paper and collaged an ocean. They returned hesitantly and asked if they could use different colours of paper for other things. I said, 'Sure, use what you need.'

Eventually, the drawing was swamped under collaged paper, and the project had morphed into something, well... experimental.

During that one experience, the child described as dependent realised that the room was full of resources and that they were at his disposal. They had always been there, but he had not been switched on to them. From then on, he moved freely around the room and was happy to join in play with different children if they were using anything he found interesting. He gained mastery over materials.

When this kind of learning takes hold, it transforms a mental structure. The 'I cannot' becomes 'this is how to do it'. Vygotsky describes how, through learning, cognitive structures can rearrange themselves, and the transformation is enduring (Vygotsky, 1986).

Assessment techniques

Your observations, conversations and interventions will reveal evidence of learning related to embedded concept experiences. How do children name and label what they are observing? How do they describe their activity with the materials or explain any relationships or transformations they observe? How do they manipulate, use and give meaning to their actions?

You can now determine whether to accept their interpretations and explanations verbatim. Their words and actions will uncover levels of knowledge and thinking. Often, children give the materials human qualities to explain phenomena, a process called anthropomorphism. They will say that a shadow moved away because it wanted to hide or that the magnet has a piece of magic in it. It is up to you where you draw the line towards more conventional knowledge.

If you decide to introduce new, conventional terms for the concepts and effects of the interaction of materials, how easily are they taken up and articulated by the children, and how keen are they to share their discoveries with their peers or with their family?

Scaffolding during mediated play experiences

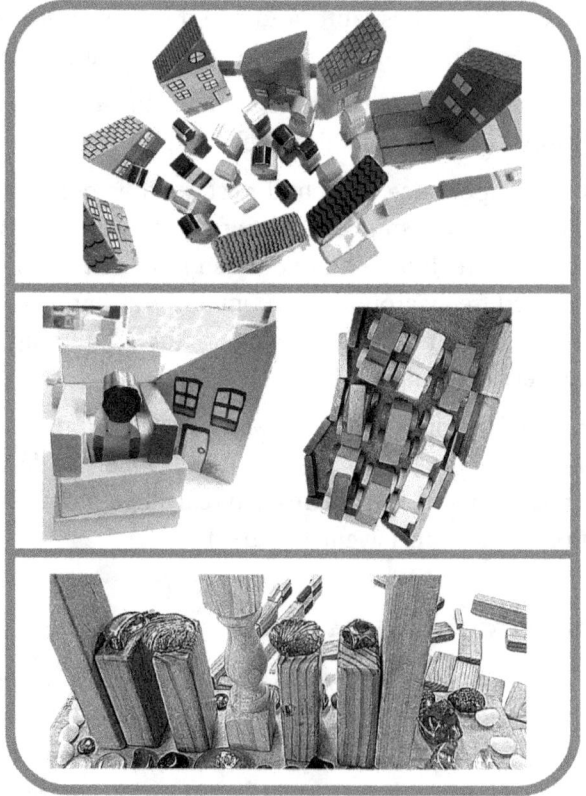

Figure 25: Small block play

Here are some sample scaffolding goals and interventions. This kind of questioning is also important in other zones:

Learning goal	Sample intervention
Enquire into a child's current knowledge and ability to express their actions	I'm really interested in what you're doing, can you tell me about it?
Provide labels the child does not know yet	What I see you doing here is putting things that are the same together. This is called sorting. You've sorted the blue, yellow and red shapes into groups that belong together. You are sorting by colour. Can you sort by shape? What would you have to do?
Expand the activity to a new level of thinking	I notice that you have enclosed all the sea animals together and all the land animals together, they each have their own habitat where they are most comfortable. I wonder where insects like to live?
Highlight thinking and metacognition	I can see you are solving a problem about how to balance your building. You've tried two different ways, which is the best?
Extend logical and creative thinking	This car you've drawn has great details. Where is it travelling to? Can you add that to your drawing?
Extend commitment and focus	The flowers you've painted are so colourful. There is space to add other parts of the flower. What else do flowers have? Do you have time to add some more details?
Provide an opportunity to change the modality	You might offer the student the opportunity to draw their block building, or construct something based on a drawing. You might ask them to create symbols for sounds they are making or narrate their story for you to capture in writing.

Often, during mediated play, you encounter exceptional creativity. A child in my group once constructed paper puppets. They were very simple. She drew two faces, each on its own A4 sheet in portrait orientation. Then, she folded the paper and used sticky tape on each doubled bottom corner to hold the fold in place. She slipped her hands into the fold and moved the paper puppets up and down to animate them.

What is remarkable is her perceptual knowledge of spatial concepts. She had drawn each face in the bottom half of each page so that the faces were the right side up when she folded it. She also folded the paper so that the faces were on the outside. All this without using trial and error. In effect, she had crafted all these spatial conversions in her mind before drawing. This is a remarkable feat for a four-year-old child.

Margaret Donaldson says:

> 'There is a distinction to be drawn between trying different actions to achieve a goal and reflecting on these as a possible set of actions before performing them. This latter activity – the planning kind – involves the temporary suspension of overt action and a turning of attention inwards upon mental acts instead. Developmentally, the course of events is from an awareness of what is without to an awareness of what is within' (Donaldson, 1984).

Mediated play is where we move the awareness from without to within.

In many classrooms, projects like these puppets are ignored or missed because we might not be looking for the conceptual understanding within them. They might not even make it to the fridge door and be discarded in the daily clean-up.

In summary

- Mediated play has a distance of three and a range of 50° (3:50°)
- A restricted range of resources are provided for students' free investigation and exploration
- Mediational scaffolding is aimed to enhance children's thinking around their independent activities
- Educators engage with students at the intersection of the child's focus and intentions related to materials
- During mediated play, teachers interact with children and provide goal-directed scaffolds to enhance customised conceptual and relational understanding
- The scaffolds relate to elevating language and labels, emphasising thinking processes, crossing modalities, extending attention span,

adding details and moving the thinking from here and now to more generalised thinking
- Educators are alert to narratives students bring to their play which can encourage further learning and creativity
- Evidence is collected through digital means like photography or video, recording conversations, capturing brief observations or using lists to check on consolidation of skills in different domains

Chapter 11
Embedded concepts

A hologram is a photographic recording of a light field rather than of an image formed by a lens, and it is used to display a fully three-dimensional image of the holographic subject.
Wikipedia (2020)

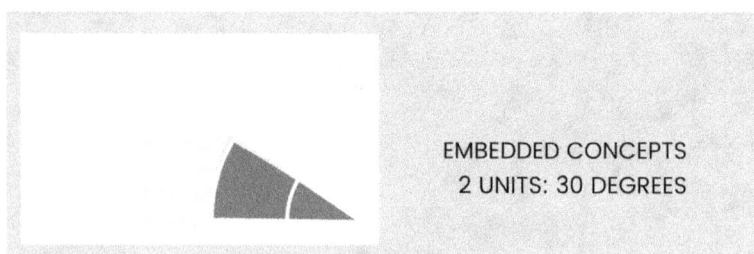

Figure 26: Embedded concepts

Coordinates

In the agility wheel for embedded concepts, the educator is at a distance of two units, and the students' range is 30° (2:30°). The balance in this configuration is weighted towards the educator's curriculum goals.

Definition

The zone of embedded concepts, whether indoors or outdoors, relates to the educator's intentional provision of resources to fuel and propel specific concept learning outcomes. Embedded concepts can be found in objects, art and construction materials, procedures, artefacts like books, or digital products like videos, photographs and video games. In this zone, we highlight what the educator selects and how the resources are deployed to animate selected conceptual learning. Within this zone, the destination is not a complete understanding of the target concept but the provision of relevant investigations that lead students towards concept clarity within a target curriculum area.

Educator's role

The educator:

- Designs learning experiences using resources and materials with embedded potential to investigate specific concepts within a target curriculum area
- Arranges the schedule and environment to invite investigation of embedded concepts
- Encourages students to develop, articulate and record their conceptual understanding
- Alerts students to the mental processes they are using as they engage with concepts
- Assesses, records and documents the learning as it emerges for the individual and the group concerning the curriculum goals

Students' role

The students:

- Focus on a curriculum concept or idea as they use and investigate the selected range of materials and resources provided by the educator
- Develop appropriate language to explain and describe the concept embedded in a task
- Construct ideas, acquire skills and develop processes and procedures related to content
- Engage in experiences and work on products related to their investigation
- Understand concepts through direct manipulation and related discussion, and be more likely to have the abstract ability to transfer the information to new contexts.

About embedded concepts

Occasionally, during a consultation, I will notice an artful array of materials. When asked why they are there, the educator often answers,

'Kids just love using them', 'I recently did a workshop on...', 'I think they add to the room's aesthetics'.

One such display was a collection of brightly coloured feathers. None of the explanations given connected the materials to anything else. They weren't connected to ideas like texture, compared to other materials, language, any particular discipline or even birds! The students' exploration was predominantly sensory and limited to the feathers.

Figure 27: Display of materials for teacher workshop

For learning to be leveraged from our resources, no matter how beautiful they are, we need to be able to answer why they are taking up room in our learning space. All materials are filled with potential, but in embedded concepts, educators must be conscious of which concepts they are surfacing and focusing on.

The potential of a pop stick

What do you see when you hold up a popsicle stick, the kind used to bring your delicious ice cream (my favourite is caramel) to your mouth?

In Reggio Emilia, educators employ the hologram metaphor, in which the smallest part of something represents the whole (Project Zero; Reggio Children, 2001, p. 59).

I love to overlay this idea when thinking about the potential of resources. Every material has latent avenues of inquiry. Before we unlock the ideas of the pop stick, it ought to be noted that the idea is not to activate all the potential but to *be aware* of the potential, to select from it what will serve the learning educators have set as a goal. We have already touched on this in mediated play.

The paddle stick starts in a white birch forest somewhere in the world, perhaps in the US or northern China. The trees are felled and transported through rugged terrains to a distant factory yard where the trunks are stacked and cured. The trunks are cut to appropriate lengths to fit a veneer-slicing machine. The wooden sections are boiled to make it easier to strip the bark manually before the logs are fed into a rotary saw to be pared into thin rolls of veneer about 600mm wide. 2.5–5.0 cubic metres of wood can be processed into veneer in an hour. The usual factory has about 50 workers. The rolls of veneer are fed through a die-cutting machine, which prints out the shape of the pop stick. The pop sticks are placed in a drying cavity, and finally, sack loads are poured into a tumbling polisher so the end product is smooth and silky to the touch. The sticks must be packaged, loaded and transported by road, rail or air to the stores where we can order or purchase them.

Pop sticks can teach through the life sciences, engineering, mathematics, geography, culture and the economy.

We have not even discussed how trees seed, grow, age, etc., let alone the opportunities for older students to study photosynthesis, transpiration, chlorophyll and changes in expiration from oxygen to carbon dioxide at night.

Apart from the potential before the pop stick is in our hands, there is the potential for what we will do with it and how students might use it to fuel their imagination.

Sticks can be used to make a photo frame because all have precise dimensions. We can use them for measuring, ruling lines, floating, counting, creating designs and making a mobile; the possibilities are endless, and a quick look on Pinterest will blow your mind.

I think you understand why I said we don't have to enact all the potential.

If you respect the potential of materials and all resources, you will consider which resources to include in your teaching to achieve your students' learning goals.

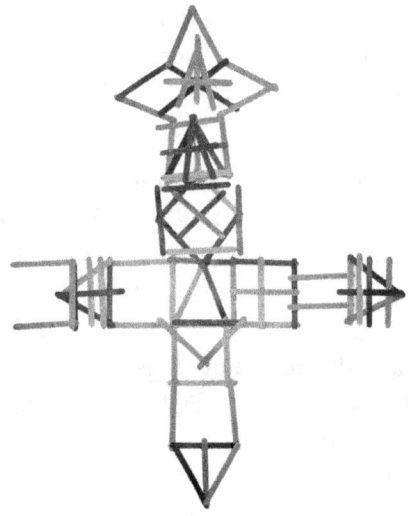

Figure 28: Pop stick sculpture

When you select materials for the embedded concepts that suit your planned curriculum, you use them convergently, i.e. together. You lead the student from the material to a predetermined destination. (This was the opposite in mediated play, where you selected divergent, i.e. different, concepts to suit the child's intentions.)

Using the latency of embedded concepts is both a science and an art. Science is knowing which concepts can be taught through a resource, and art is imagining what they might reveal when children use the knowledge they gain from them.

Embedded concepts are a means of attuning students to information without telling them directly. They make the concepts discoverable.

One of the well-researched ideas about efficient, flexible learning is that concepts are more easily and permanently understood if they are encountered in a variety of situations (Kilpatrick et al., 2001). Students gather the data and see what is behaving the same way. What is general or translatable across each of the situations?

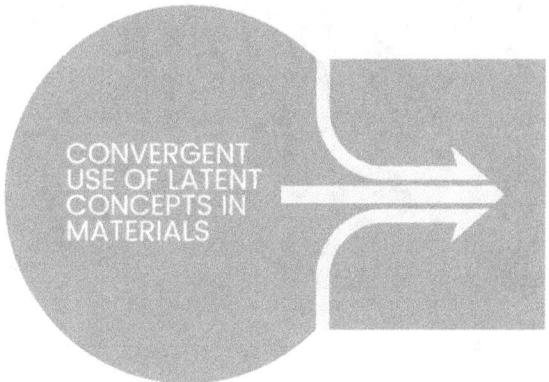

Figure 29: Convergent use of latent concepts

Resourcing for embedded concepts

As with any other plan, the goal will drive your selection of resources. There are two main ways of presenting them: multiple investigation areas drawing out the same concept or a single investigation area with several choices related to the target concept.

A range of connected experiences across time and space

States of water

The Explorations project discussed in Chapter 4 lasted an entire semester. Water investigations, specifically, drawing out knowledge of the states of water, solid, liquid and gas, occurred over time in several different investigation areas. Ice was included so that the melting and refreezing could be investigated.

Figure 30: Exploration of states of water

We used water in the liquid form in a water tray with several jugs, containers, tubes of different diameters and funnels. We provided water on tables with pipettes and eyedroppers where children could put drops of water onto different materials. The idea was to introduce the concept of absorbency of materials and whether and how efficiently they might contain water. We asked them to make the smallest piece of water they could.

In a group activity one day, in the safest possible way, water was boiled in an electric frying pan, and a cold metal surface was held above the steam for droplets to condense onto. We didn't expect all the children to understand fully the condensation process, but the entire water cycle was embedded in different materials and processes over time.

We put water into balloons for children to feel that the shape of the water was changing. We provided vessels for pouring from narrow to wide, and wide to narrow containers to explore what happened to the volume.

The experiences listed here are skewed towards the sciences, but as you read in Chapter 4, the arts, cultural narrative, dance and music were also used to explore water. The meanings were about water and our relationship with, reliance on, appreciation of and imagination regarding this miraculous element.

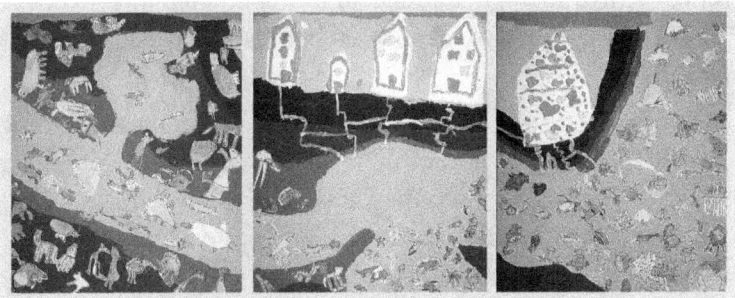

Figure 31: 'Uses of water' triptych

Figure 32: Exploration of Australia's First People's' art

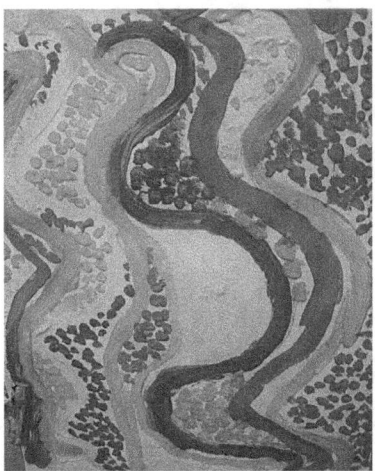

Figure 33: Representation of rainbow serpent

Magnetism

You could do the same by embedding magnetism in several ways across your room or offering students several different encounters with it over time. Most classrooms have metal whiteboards and use magnets daily to secure display materials.

If you are keen for a student to know the different qualities of magnets, such as which materials attract them or that a magnet has two polar opposites, you focus directly on the knowledge you want your students to learn. You provide a magnet, cardboard and supporting materials. They predict which materials will move above the cardboard as the magnet moves below. The students refine their knowledge and understand that metal objects can be moved, not wooden, plastic or paper, etc.

To learn about polar opposites, you purposely select north and south bar magnets to develop that knowledge. The intention for the learning is essential to the task. The students' investigations have them observe the effect of polarity to see the forces at work.

This early experience sets students up later to explain the role of magnetism in electricity and how electromagnetism is used as a power source. It will enable them to understand the role of polarity in how solutions move around the human body. One encounter with magnets, or encounters without discussion about what is occurring, will not have them progressively understand this universally applicable force. This extends to understanding that your views about life can be the polar opposite of someone else's.

In embedded learning, students develop a deep understanding of concepts because the materials are supported by both sensory information and intentional language. They hear terminology in context, and explaining what they are observing makes sense because they have directly engaged with the materials. They are given time to consolidate new language and advance their curriculum understanding.

Several activities related to a concept in one investigation area

Alternatively, to provide experiences across several areas, you might set up one area with different materials to extract the same information. One such example was a light exploration area, where we provided an overhead projector and screen with selected materials because they were transparent, translucent, opaque and combinations of those qualities for children to explore.

Beside it, on a table, we also placed a piece of Perspex up to about 25cm on blocks with white paper below and provided mini torches. The children shone the torches over materials on the Perspex, creating shadows and reflections on the paper below. They learnt to change the size of the shadows by moving the torch further away or closer to the materials. They created complex shadows by using two torches. The information was further mobilised when the children made a story and a shadow play. Their knowledge enabled them to control the size of the shadows on the screen.

In this example, you see how the potential of embedded concepts is multiplied by lining up several objects so that they act on one another. They can use the relationships between the objects to solve problems or achieve effects.

This exploration was captivating to both children's curiosity and imagination and, over time, the experience made them intensely aware of light and shadow, one of the most observable sciences available to us. When learning becomes complex, it is because several things act together. So, embedding information in this way allows the children to experience the effect and begin to unpack the relationships and the role of the different elements in what is happening.

Highlight thinking around embedded concepts

The emphasis is not only on labelling the objects and interactions with the materials, but also on the students' thinking processes in acquiring new knowledge.

Teachers can lay the foundation for students to use their metacognitive capacity.

For example, if you want them to have sound scientific knowledge, you can gradually introduce the methodology of forming hypotheses, observing patterns, recording data, reviewing information and framing questions. These scientific inquiry skills are needed as a foundation for biological, chemical and all other sciences. This is done at the appropriate level.

When you offer an activity with large PVC pipes and things that roll, like marbles, ping pong balls, etc., you ask: 'What are you going to test out today? Which will roll further, the ping pong or golf ball? How can you measure how far they go? Wow, why do you think that happened? What happens if the pipe is set up more steeply against the sofa? Why do you think so? Will the balls go faster, further? Would you like to draw your experiment to explain it to your friends?' Your materials allow you to surface vocabulary, relationship thinking and procedures like the scientific method.

You might record when children use words and phrases like noticed, explained, remembered, thought that if I did x then y, tried out, learned, compared, thought about, grouped, planned, changed my idea and any other process words discussed in earlier chapters. You can also be alert for theory of mind, where they attribute a thought, idea, plan or change of idea to other children in the group. Children often say, 'First, Daniel thought the heartbeat went slow when you ran; then, when we measured, he changed his mind'. This is evidence that children are recognising metacognition in others.

When embedding concepts, we aren't imposing an out-of-context, episodic task and expecting the students to learn and memorise dislocated information. The connections and relationships are clear to them, and they can transfer the knowledge because they thoroughly understand both the content and the mental processes they used to obtain it.

This chapter has focused heavily on scientific concepts. However, the literacy and art materials you provide can equally surface abstract concepts like friendship, happiness, loyalty, responsibility, power, beauty, imagination or love. These concepts can be investigated and explored equally. Stories, poems, letters, puppetry, drama and cultural celebrations contain latent concepts for marvellous investigations. I will leave you to design investigations to extract these and the one million other concepts you can think of.

In summary

- Activating learning using embedded concepts has the teacher at a distance of two units and the student applying a 30° range of independent choice (2:30°)
- Embedded concepts are used when the educator selects specific materials and employs them strategically so that students can discover them, not be directly taught

- Materials, procedures, artefacts or excursions and incursions are selected because they provide inroads to understanding concepts without employing direct teaching
- Students benefit from observing, manipulating and experiencing the concept embedded, either as a single entity, such as a shape, or as something being acted on by other environmental elements, such as heat or temperature on ice or light on shadows
- Embedded materials provide meaningful contexts and experiences to introduce abstract and transferable ideas such as temperature, magnetism, texture or symmetry. They are also a way to introduce concepts such as trust, friendship, optimism and other abstract ideas through literature and other means
- Educators can track and record children's language progress, and their ability to recognise thinking processes and metacognitive language, and explain different relationships within and among other materials
- The potential of materials and situations to unlock learning is always present

Chapter 12

Clarity of concept

Music is powered by ideas. If you don't have clarity of ideas, you're just communicating sheer sound.

Yo-Yo Ma – cellist

Figure 34: Concept clarity

Coordinates

The clarity of concept learning zone is the closest proximity to students with the most specific educator goals and the most restricted choice of activity for students (1:25°).

Definition

The clarity of concept zone is a space where the objective is full comprehension and understanding. It is not time-restricted, so comprehension does not need to be reached in a day; it can be a process. We expect students to achieve full understanding, not just move towards it. Clarity of concept means complete comprehension. While the zone isn't time restricted, and understanding can develop over time, the goal is to reach clarity within this zone. This is crucial when foundational concepts are needed to support more complex ideas. The destination is the clarity of the concept. This is especially important when a base concept is required to support more complex ideas.

Educator's role

The educator:

- Designs learning experiences using processes, resources and materials to ensure a student understands the target concept
- Arranges the schedule and environment so that students learn and mobilise a concept or group of related concepts
- Encourages students to apply, articulate and record their conceptual understanding
- Alerts students to the mental processes they are using as they master concepts
- Assesses, records and documents the learning as it emerges for the individual and the group to achieving concept clarity

Students' role

The students:

- Focus on and develop comprehensive understanding of a specific curriculum concept or cluster of concepts
- Acquire appropriate language to identify, define, use and communicate target curriculum concepts
- Can deploy knowledge of concepts in application tasks
- Generate products that demonstrate and communicate their understanding of the learned concepts

About clarity of concept

The difference between working on clarity and the three zones I have already discussed is that we don't want to work towards conceptual understanding or creating the pathway as before; we want the concept to land. We want evidence that a student has the required knowledge to move on to something more complex. This is the most prescriptive configuration of the seven zones.

The goal is understanding of the concept, but this does not mean we have to be prescriptive in how the information is presented. We can use the most direct approach and tell students what they need to learn or choose a more roundabout approach.

Even in this most proximal zone, we can distinguish between a child learning in a rote fashion or learning to understand. Rote learning can be helpful in enabling a student to achieve a task quickly and efficiently without fully understanding why the rote information is valid. Learning the times tables is an example of how simply having the answers immediately to hand saves time, effort and anguish. Using rote knowledge, formulas and rules in many situations successfully generates correct answers. They are shortcuts. In some cases, this is extremely helpful. But sometimes, without a complete understanding, there is a ceiling the student will reach beyond which their knowledge is inadequate for the complexity of a task.

If at all possible, it is essential for students to genuinely understand the concepts.

The kind of teaching using formulas and rules is called instrumental, and the kind where concepts are understood is called relational. Both are necessary, but they are different.

Reaching clarity through instrumental or relational teaching

Have you ever considered a clock as a number line? If you have, you were many years ahead of me. I was fortunate to attend a maths workshop on the difference between instrumental and relational teaching methods.

Instrumental teaching emphasises procedures and rules, and gives the students practice tasks to apply them.

Relational teaching aims to uncover the conceptual reasons that underpin the rules (Skemp, 1986).

Back to the clock. For the first time in this workshop, I mentally opened a circle with numbers on it and converted it to a linear format: a number line from 1 to 12. It doesn't sound like much, but it was a conceptual revelation. I loved the flexibility of a circular number line.

In this workshop, there were other revelatory ideas. For the first time, I derived the features of a prism for myself. Before this, I had incorrectly conceptualised a cone as a prism. If you are a consummate mathematician – and you're laughing now, I don't mind. It was so exciting to me that *I had clarified my thinking.*

We want students to achieve clarity, but we can't give it to them. They have to construct it. Our educational culture commonly packages and presents information to students using a direct teaching methodology. This may be precisely what they need, but sometimes, it prevents the student from actively thinking and learning about the topic. They focus exclusively on what the teacher presents and aren't motivated to explore it or make spontaneous connections between it and related knowledge. They get used to being provided with packaged information. It is like fast food for thinking; they sidestep doing slow, integrative thinking. Hopefully, you will recall the earlier conversation about how understanding length, ratio and the term 'circumference' are essential for understanding pi.

In relational teaching, more emphasis is placed on conceptual and structural information than on rules and procedures. Of course, you need both. But if students can understand the basis of the rules, so much the better. It is good to keep both in mind when we plan activities.

Relational teaching can be a focus in the early years

I am so excited about the value of relational teaching. It can be widely used in the early years because we have the time to work on concepts in various ways, indoors and outdoors.

Taking time over new concepts

Recognising a concept operating in diverse contexts proves that you fully understand it. But to get to the stage of recognising and employing concepts in this flexible way, you must first be clear about the concept's meaning.

Something that often happens when teaching a new piece of information is that not enough time is spent consolidating it, or too few examples or encounters are provided to illustrate it before moving on.

Earlier, I spoke about selective association, discrimination and generalisation. In the last, selective generalisation, students can pick concepts and how they work in a very flexible way, but they will only do this if they know what something is and what it is made up of. So first, you have to build clarity.

Most knowledge is dependent on other knowledge

Having clarity is especially vital when knowledge builds in layers or networks. If you don't understand division, will you know fractions? If you don't understand fractions, numerators and denominators, what are your chances of understanding variables in fractions in algebra?

Many children move through school from one year to another with gaps in their knowledge. In the early years, vocabulary and language structures can be successfully taught in engaging, informal ways. You can actively introduce knowledge that is the foundation of a conceptual framework for life.

Clarity of thought is important in many mathematical concepts

So much knowledge is about measuring things in different ways. We can scaffold this knowledge in our talking aloud. We can talk about cutting things in half. Having half a piece of paper, changing partners halfway to the playground, reading half the book now and half later. When the students understand halves, you can ask them to estimate how much water they need to fill half a container. You are establishing a concept of proportion. Sticking with halves until children know the idea will make moving on to quarters easier. Some adults at college think 1 over 8 is more than 1 over 4. Clearly, the idea of proportions and fractions never fully landed!

Mary Baratta-Lorton, in her excellent book *Mathematics Their Way*, advocates giving children multiple ways to solve a particular task or problem (Baratta-Lorton, 1994). They are encouraged to use illustrations, representations, drawings, diagrams, manipulative materials and small group discussions to solve problems. Block practice and drills can be used, and repetitive practice can be effective, but drills without comprehension are not long-lasting.

According to the Erikson Institute, children must master five critical concepts to be successful at mathematical thinking over time:

1. **One-to-one correspondence.** This is the principle that every object will have a corresponding number in a collection of objects.
2. **Stable order principle.** You have to say the counting words in the same order every time.
3. **The cardinal principle.** The trick that the last word you say is the total amount. In a group, if you've counted 1, 2, 3 – the total number in the group is three. Cardinality is the absolute value of a number.
4. **The abstract principle.** The principle means that if you have three things in a group, no matter which one you count first, regardless of

their colour, shape or size, there are still three in the group. It is the conservation of constancy of numbers.

5. **Order irrelevance.** It doesn't matter which member of a group you count in which order; you still get the same total.

Children will learn over time that number is used in three ways:

1. **Ordinal number** – this relates to the sequence of things: first, second, third, last, etc.
2. **Cardinal number** – as discussed above, this is the absolute value of the number.
3. **Nominative number** – this number names something or identifies it, for example, your house number, raffle ticket or telephone number. It has nothing to do with the value of a number.

Neither preschoolers nor perhaps certain-level primary children need to know this terminology, but as educators, we need to know what we are working towards for later mathematical success.

I recommend using an online children's maths dictionary to check on any of your maths facts – try www.amathsdictionaryforkids.com.

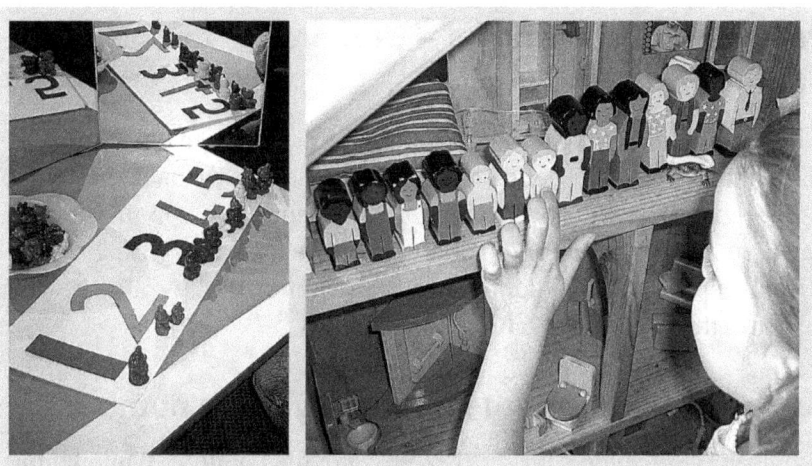

Figure 35: One-to-one correspondence

Knowledge gaps need to be addressed

At the beginning of teaching a concept, or if students have already investigated topics, ideas and concepts and still do not understand them, you must find ways to consolidate them. Concrete materials, videos, actions, peer teaching or narrative are avenues to construct clarity.

One great strategy in the early years is to use the human body as a teaching mechanism!

Embodied cognition – 'I like to move it move it!'

There is a kind of cognition called embodied cognition. Since time began, we have used our bodies and our perspective to think about and define abstract things (Falikman, 2014). For instance, we see the future as *ahead* of us and the past as *behind* us. We say things like on the one *hand*, x, and on the other, y. We talk about having a future *vision*, doing an about-*face*, setting a *pace*, having a stiff upper *lip* and making a quantum *leap*.

Drama, outdoor activities and awareness of the body in space can often be a means to develop an understanding of complex abstract ideas. Forming a square, circle or oval shape; standing at equidistant intervals; measuring activities like the number of bunny hops in one minute or the heartbeat before and after a one-minute-long sprint are all ways to enable students to engage with abstract concepts. Still, in a way, their bodies are involved.

Personal is meaningful – personal is the basis of general

When each child's height measurement is graphed on a long paper strip bar graph beside their friend's on the wall in the classroom, there is a good chance that they understand there is a difference between their number and their friend's number. You don't even have to use the term 'bar graph'. The concept is about the difference in the number they counted, which relates to the concepts of more, equal and less.

Adjust measurements to manageable numbers

You need to set some concepts to the age of the children. When younger children want to measure their height or how long their line of blocks is, don't reach for a ruler with centimetres. Have the children look around the room for something to measure with. Ideally, they will choose something regular, like a pop stick or a drinking straw. If they don't, you might like to go into the kind of discussion I mentioned earlier about precision and agreement of measurements.

The longer the measuring tool, the more likely the children will observe and understand the measuring process. Centimetres are too fine a measure to begin with and the numbers are too big for early maths learners.

When we measured children's heartbeats because they wanted to know if they got faster or slower when they ran for a minute, we didn't use the actual heartbeat but divided it by four or five to get a number children could easily understand, record and compare.

As discussed before, recording conversations and using different digital means can capture the children's ideas, investigations and products.

Clarity and emotion

Students very quickly come adrift if they don't understand a task. I have mentioned before the inextricable link between cognition and emotion. If there is stress around cognition, it will turn into emotion. You might see a child acting out, being a class clown, withdrawing, blocking, avoiding, being evasive or even having difficulty.

In an article on thresholds of learning, Sarah Doenmez writes:

> 'Learning is about knowledge and skills, but it is also inextricably tied to our perceptions of ourselves. As we face cognitive challenges, we also face challenges to our identity. When we can't quickly resolve these challenges, we are unmoored and drift in a "liquid space." This is the place of liminality. It can be a place of danger or an adventure; it can drown or nourish learning' (Doenmez, 2020).

Knowledge thresholds

New knowledge is always at a threshold. If it is at the upper limit of the child's current knowledge, they might feel confused or anxious. It can be a point where they develop negative emotions about learning, about particular kinds of learning and, worse, about themselves. If we sacrifice the student's understanding to speed ahead to complete a curriculum goal, we miss the point entirely. From 1911, the words of Sister Jane Erskine Stuart make sense:

> '...each mind needs to be met just where it is – with its own mental images, vocabulary, habit of thought and attention, all calling for consideration and adaptation of the subject to their particular case...' (Stuart, 1911).

Sometimes, we must go backwards to go forward. We meet the students where they are and scaffold upwards and outwards from there. To do this, we must know where they are.

Clarity of concept also applies when there is a learning task that you would like all the students to achieve in a specific way. This is often appropriate at the primary level, where children need full competence with literacy, maths or other concepts, which form the basis of later, more abstract tasks. In the early years, self-regulation skills, motor skills and foundation concepts are needed to move on to later schooling. In these situations, we might use, dare I say it, a worksheet or an identical task. (I'm waiting to be struck down by lightning.)

Concept clarity needs persistence. It might include verbal telling, repetition and demonstration, but use different modalities when working at this stage. Make it hands-on and use concrete equipment if necessary. With some students, the educator may need to go back to mediated learning if the task or understanding is outside the child's zone of proximal development (Bodrova & Leong, 1996).

In summary

- Clarity of concept is a learning zone with the closest proximity of the educator and the narrowest goal selection for students (1:25°)
- The intention in this zone is for the student to completely understand the content, a skill or a mental process
- It is preferable for students not to rely on procedures and rules (instrumental learning) without understanding the conceptual and structural principles that underlie the rules (relational learning). Educators benefit from being aware of both
- The student should be capable of explaining the knowledge, and it should be committed to long-term memory and part of their knowledge portfolio
- If the student has not internalised the necessary information, steps should be taken to ensure they do. This might mean changing modalities, going back a few steps, creating more encounters or giving it more time

Chapter 13
Closed-ended mobilisation

'Begin with the end in mind' is based on the principle that all things are created twice. There's a mental or first creation, and a physical or second creation to all things.

Steven Covey

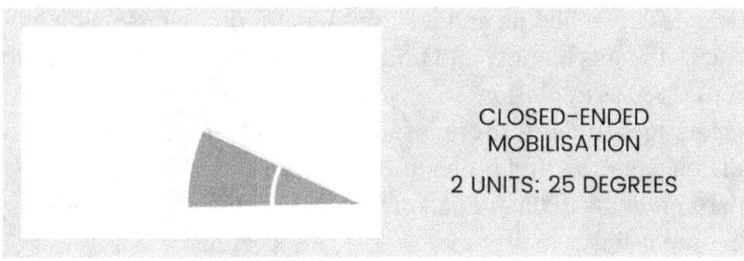

Figure 36: Closed-ended mobilisation

Coordinates

Closed-ended mobilisation has the educator at two units and the student's range of choice at 25° (2:25°). There is a sense of equivalence in this zone where the educator and student work shoulder to shoulder.

Definition

Closed-ended knowledge mobilisation occurs when students are asked to use what they have learned to achieve a predictable and predetermined goal. Beyond understanding a concept, process, idea or symbol, the task is to combine multiple elements to complete a task. Closed-ended mobilisation is the application, elaboration or deployment of knowledge towards a predetermined destination.

The term 'closed-ended' is often judged negatively in education analysis. However, when we examine the idea, we see that much of what is done in preschool and primary settings is closed-ended, and it is necessary. We regularly want students to arrive at a specific destination because it means they have internalised the knowledge we want them to consolidate.

The emphasis is equally on the goal students reach and the process they design and navigate to achieve it. Closed-ended methods are only limiting if we teach a single path or offer one modality to reach the destination.

Educator's role

The educator:

- Designs learning experiences using processes, resources and materials so that students accomplish a predictable or predetermined outcome
- Arranges the schedule and environment for problem-solving in which students identify and understand the task and sequence the steps towards a solution
- Encourages students to apply, articulate and record their problem-solving strategies and procedures
- Alerts students to the mental processes, routines and procedures they are using as they work towards closed-ended goals
- Includes flexibility and alternative means of reaching a single goal
- Assesses, records and documents the processes and procedures as the individual and the group implement them to achieve the known goal

Students' role

The students:

- Focus on a task and apply their knowledge to solve a problem or reach a predetermined learning goal
- Develop appropriate procedures and sequence steps to complete tasks
- Use appropriate language to communicate their processes and outcomes
- Generate products that demonstrate and communicate their understanding of the learned concept

About closed-ended mobilisation

Closed-ended tasks don't have to be repetitive and boring. Indeed, there is evidence that the more varied and exciting the problems or tasks related to one concept are, the better children internalise the principles (Ben-Hur, 2006). During problem-solving towards closed-ended goals, different kinds of knowledge are mobilised.

To solve problems, students need several abilities:

- Practice with various problem types
- Skills to identify and understand the problem
- Recognise language that indicates different maths or other subject operations
- Adjust methods to reach the correct solution

The problem-solving process involves pattern identification and recognising a recurring sequence.

Below are five examples of how students benefit from closed-ended tasks. The examples emphasise that there is more than one way to reach a target and that understanding the problem-solving processes is crucial.

Example one

When we teach children to write, they must reproduce the letters correctly at some point. We don't need to be prescriptive at the start of the journey. In preschool or primary settings, you can offer choices. The shape of the letter is a given, but students can write shapes in the air, trace them in sand or create them with modelling clay.

Example two

One morning, when my four-year-olds arrived in my classroom, all the play equipment was strewn across the carpet. It was a mega-sorting challenge. Everyone was a detective, choosing what they were looking for. They gathered their chosen items and placed them back where they belonged in the room.

After the activity, a comprehensive discussion was held about the importance of order, role allocation and the benefits of knowing the location of items. This discussion played a significant role in reinforcing the learning. Next, the experience was extended to their visits to the supermarket. Where would they find the ice lollies, and why?

Consolidate information before introducing flexible thinking

Example three

When we want children to use numeric knowledge, we set a task. Depending on their comprehension level, the task should be challenging enough for children to achieve but not be outside their grasp. As indicated several times in this book, ensure children have the base knowledge before you extend knowledge. Develop children's ability to use equations, problems and tasks by consolidating them using one concept at a time. This consolidation of expertise is key to building a secure and confident learning foundation.

There is no space to show an example of long division here, and I know it's not part of the early years syllabus, but, like pi, I am using it to demonstrate how complex some learning is for children. In long division, a complex pattern of actions is required. You must:

- Multiply the divisor
- Subtract the product from the whole dividend
- Draw down the next digit
- Repeat the steps in this problem-solving environment to achieve the outcome

I am sure you see that the language may be beyond the comprehension of many primary students. They need to consolidate the terminology before they can do the sums.

Long division also requires spatial concepts:

- Where do you write the digits?
- Consider directionality – do you start your operation on the left or right?
- Do you write above or below the line?
- Monitor where you are within these complex processes

Thankfully, we do not do long divisions in the early years of the classroom, but students start to develop academic know-how. They have many opportunities to develop neural networks for understanding words and patterns. As they do this, they create the competence they will need to recognise patterns, follow processes and hold information in short-term memory to achieve a purpose.

Example four

You can make your closed-ended tasks more open-ended in character.

You might tell students, 'You've done this challenging sum: 23 + 16 = 37. (I am just checking if you are asleep!) 23 +16 = 39. Can you make seven sums that add up to 39? Now, can you make a subtraction sum with the answer 39?'

Similar tasks are:

'If I asked you to make six shades of orange, how could you do that?'

'You have learned now that mixing yellow and red makes orange. How can you create an instruction for your friend to mix exactly the same orange colour as you?'

Example five

Word problems are harder than simple equations because they include extraneous information. For example, numeric addition combines two numbers to find the total. In a word problem, students must determine which details to use and which to ignore. This makes solving word problems more challenging.

For example, two sisters, Emma and Janet, had 10 lollies each. Emma's lollies were yellow, and Janet's lollies were pink. They shared all their lollies among four cousins who were visiting them. How many lollies did each of the visiting cousins get?

There is a procedure for problem-solving:
- Define the problem
- Determine which elements are relevant
- Visualise the steps
- Sequence the steps
- Enact the steps
- Reach the conclusion
- Record the information

Children learn from peers and errors

When children approach challenges and reflect on their processes and procedures, they learn from one another's thinking mechanisms, plans and workings. Most importantly, you and they will learn from their mistakes. If they make mistakes when they apply, transpose and transform information during their workings, it gives clues about what might need reinforcement. Simply marking an error and providing a child with the correct answer won't enable you to drill down to correct a misconception.

It is advantageous when students work on the same task. They share what they found easy, what was tricky and how they overcame a particular hurdle. They highlight which processes or ideas did not serve them, which strategy they employed and how they would do it next time.

Children love having ownership of their way of doing things. You'll hear things like, 'It was my idea to use the bottle cap to measure the exact amount of white paint.'

'Yes, and it was Ella's idea to use the cotton bud to get all the paint out so that it was the whole amount and none was left in the cap.'

Challenge students after they have consolidated their knowledge

Reversibility

During closed-ended problems, once children are familiar with a concept, you might introduce reversibility and opposites to test the durability of the knowledge. You might also change the perspective and make them the judges! Ask them to select from several products and evaluate them according to what they know.

Set challenges

'You have built a one-storey building in the shape of a square. Can you do one shaped like a triangle?'

'You have spent ages learning how to write an excellent sentence. Now I want you to write a really bad one, swap it with a friend and try to make each other's excellent again. Get together and explain what you have done and why.'

The art of interleaving tasks

You might be familiar with evidence that interleaving (mixing up the kinds of tasks) is better for learning, retention and recall than giving a block of the same type of exercise. And you are correct. However, the interleaving should only be done once the children fully understand each of the concepts you'd like to interleave for practising. They must know something well before interleaving begins. Interleaving is a second layer, not an initial practice, of concept consolidation (Horvath, 2019; Epstein, 2019).

The reason the interleaving works once each concept is established is the spontaneous comparisons that have to be made as each new task is presented. The student gains fluency with adapting their thinking, skill or procedure for each new task in the interleaved sequence.

As you can see, closed-ended mobilisation is an extremely valuable learning zone. Spending time unpacking problems into steps with students and evaluating efficiency is as important as solving the tasks correctly. Discovering different ways of doing things builds flexibility in their thinking. It helps students learn the skills and knowledge they need to implement the more challenging zone of open-ended mobilisation.

In summary

- Closed-ended mobilisation is the setting of tasks at various levels of challenge that have a known outcome
- Solving the challenge may be done directly and using one pathway, but it is possible to introduce flexibility and multiple ways to solve the problem or task
- Students do well if they are alerted to the cues central to framing problems
- It is important to practise breaking complex tasks down into steps and sequencing the steps clearly before expecting children to employ them without discussion
- Students are at an advantage if they can identify the problem. Once they are comfortable identifying problems offered in block practice, it's beneficial to interleave different kinds of problems so children can identify them more easily
- Students benefit from discussing their ideas, processes, mistakes, procedures, strategies, hurdles and possible improvements with others. This also allows them to observe and use others' thoughts and methods

Chapter 14
Open-ended mobilisation

You don't think your way to creative work. You work your way to creative thinking.'
George Nelson – architect and designer

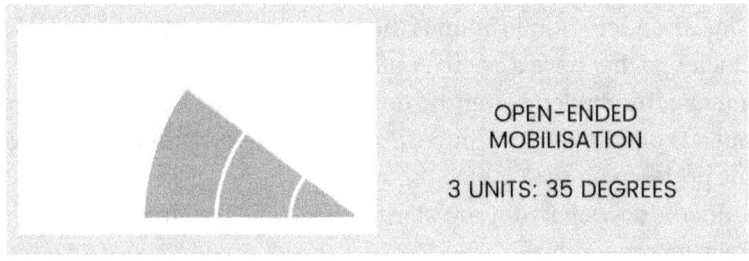

Figure 37: Open-ended mobilisation

Coordinates

Open-ended mobilisation has the educator at three units and the students' range at 35° (3:35°).

Definition

Open-ended mobilisation of knowledge is when students are inspired and encouraged to activate their curricular learning in novel and exciting ways. Beyond where a concept, process, idea or symbol is understood, the task is to combine multiple elements towards an unrestricted outcome or destination. The goal is visualised by the individual or a collaborative group of students to use, represent and communicate their knowledge in more personal ways than in closed-ended mobilisation. Students have greater freedom in acquiring, capturing, recording and communicating their understanding. The zone is not total creativity, as in the final zone (auto-generative creativity). In open-ended mobilisation, the creative goal remains within the curriculum or project-based parameters. As in closed-ended problem-solving, in open-ended mobilisation, emphasis is equally on the *process* students use to inspect, design and achieve their goal, as it is on the *product* they create or enact.

Educator's role

The educator:

- Designs learning experiences using processes, resources and materials so that students can acquire, activate and communicate their knowledge in a variety of ways
- Arranges the schedule and environment for individual or collaborative research and planning towards a visualised product or destination
- Encourages students to define, analyse, sequence and plan the steps to achieve and communicate their chosen path and destination
- Encourages students to apply, articulate and record their creative thinking, problem-solving strategies and procedures
- Alerts students to the mental processes, routines and procedures they are using as they work towards open-ended goals
- Emphasises flexibility and the testing of alternative means of reaching a creative goal
- Assesses, records and documents the processes and procedures as the individual and the group implement them to achieve their outcomes

Students' role

The students:

- Harness and apply their knowledge to project a personal or collaborative means of representing and communicating their curriculum learning and understanding
- Develop appropriate plans and procedures, and sequence the steps to complete their self-designed tasks

- Use appropriate language, be it verbal or non-verbal, to communicate their processes and outcomes
- Use knowledge of concepts and apply it to achieve their visualised goal
- Generate a range of outcomes and products that demonstrate and communicate their understanding of learned concepts

About open-ended mobilisation

In open-ended mobilisation, there is still a curriculum goal for the learning. Even so, the end product is open-ended, giving students a choice in acquiring, planning, traversing, reaching and reporting their conceptual understanding. There is increased freedom in the pathways, destinations, processes and communication of learning.

I will use the example of a curriculum task presented by six teenage girls in a Year 9 literature classroom at an art, ballet, music and drama school where I began my career in education. I know it is outside of our immediate age group, but the principle holds.

> In the room, first, one high, heavenly note trilling. Then a slow, sinuous fall into lower, fuller tones. The resonating voice advances and retreats. It rounds unexpectedly into haunting minor tones. The heart retracts and aches. The room seems to darken. Now new voices: from every corner, every space. Some high, some low, some long, some sighing, some a stuck slow staccato. The chorus builds, assaulting the listener from every side. Then, each in its own time, the voices begin their retreat. Sequential silence. You feather down and settle as the last sound recedes...

I was 'teaching' Samuel Taylor Coleridge's *The Rime of the Ancient Mariner*, which, as you might know, was written in a language that was not easily accessible to the group when they first encountered it. But we worked through it by creating access points from their own experience.

In one part of Coleridge's epic poem, marooned sailors hear haunting voices in the air. I asked the girls who specialised in music if they would work together to enact these stanzas. Suffice it to say that their performance exceeded my expectations. Their fellow students and I were transfixed by their work and their creativity. In an entirely new way, the poem was 'taught' to me.

Learning the poem was compulsory in a set curriculum, but the students and I had freedom about how we could do it. Like closed-ended projects, open-ended tasks require procedures. The difference is that the exact outcome is unknown to everyone at the start. The unifying idea is the content learning you are aiming to cover.

If not with music, you can start in the early years with Unifix blocks. 'Use these Unifix blocks and teach me and your friends things you know about numbers.'

'Let's go outside in the sunshine today and see what the shadows are doing.'

A school I visited a few years ago could hardly get their students into the classrooms in the morning. Not one, but four year levels of children from K4 through Year 2 were infatuated with shadows. Not only the standard kind where an object blocks the sun, but an immense variety of shadows and reflections.

The educators had been keen to introduce a science module in the Year 1 and 2 groups and chose light and shadow because, as I've indicated before, it is a highly observable science.

The teachers didn't only rely on what was already available in the space outdoors, like plants, play equipment, etc. to cast shadows, but also strung up some washing lines between different poles and trees. They pegged up many different sizes and colours of laminated translucent paper like tissue paper, cellophane and patterned papers, some with cut-out shapes. They strung up fabric in places where light was coming in from more than one direction. In one spot, light was coming from inside a building through a window into the playground and directly from the sun. This complicated and multiplied the shadows.

The kids were more than excited about the density of the shadows, how dark they were, the multitude of shadows, the opacity, translucency and transparency of shadows. Among the coloured outdoor sheets and mobiles, there were also examples of foil and reflective surfaces.

The children involved in the project had younger siblings at the school, and the younger children also got involved in the exploration. In a safe concrete area as parents were dropping students off at school, they saw kids drawing around others' shadows using chalk and recording their names within them. The plan was to come out later in the day, stand in the 'shadow footprints,' and see where the shadows had moved to.

In the classroom, children were invited to explain what they had observed and outline the experiments they wanted to do the following week.

Figure 38: Light exploration

After several weeks of investigations, children were invited to use what they knew to do their light projects in the Year 1 and Year 2 classes. Some children wrote shadow plays and made shadow puppets; others created light collages with different materials on a light projector which they photographed for a 'light gallery'.

A group of children took photographs throughout the day and recorded the lengths and angles of the shadows as they moved. They produced a book, *A Story of Moving Shadows*.

One group of children, who had loved the coloured shadows, decided to give each colour a musical note, and they selected five colours. The music was played on resonator bells. Resonator bells can be played like a xylophone, except each sound is a separate 'bell', so the notes can be shared, and children can use one or more at a time. The 'bells' are based on the pentatonic scale. On this five-note scale, all the sounds are harmonious. So, it didn't matter which bell was played in which order to get a lovely sound.

The children had strips of colour lined up in different orders to play the different melodies. Five children each had a bell, which they would play when their colour came up. A 'conductor' pointed at the 'notes'.

Someone suggested that the sounds could be repeated, so they cut out multiple strips of each colour. A blue or any colour's sound could be repeated several times before moving on to another sound. Another child suggested the music could be sped up or slowed down. So, the spaces between the paper strip notes indicated more time before the next note.

This added more variety to the compositions. One of the discoveries was that the melodies could be identically repeated if the patterns were repeated. The music was recorded and could be replayed. It was an astounding project for Year 1 and Year 2 children. It was a musical composition using colour as notation. It controlled the pitch, pattern and timing of the melodies. And it was based on light!

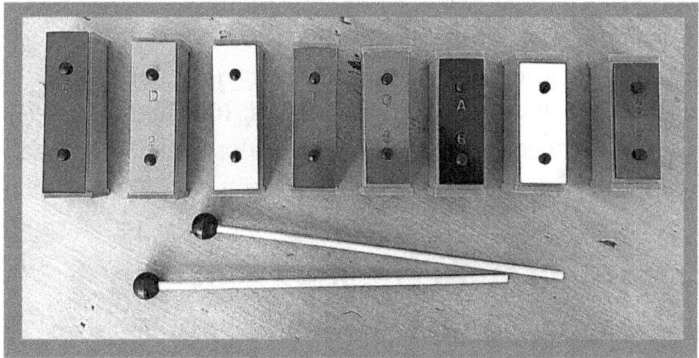

Figure 39: Resonator bells

There are many prompts outside that can inspire creativity. How about the question, 'How can we get the wind to help us make beautiful sounds?' The creative projects don't need to be as extensive as the ones above.

Matchstick pattern wrapping paper

Like pop sticks, most classrooms have natural matchsticks (without the graphite flint).

I started an experience saying, 'I'm giving everyone five matchsticks today. Make a pattern using all five and then draw it onto paper. When it is recorded, break your pattern and make a new one. When you've made as many patterns as you want to, use your patterns to make beautiful wrapping paper for next week's family day. You can use any art materials in the studio to put your designs on the wrapping paper.'

Sister Jane Erskine Stuart, a Catholic Educator in 1911, wrote:

> '...we are beginning to believe what has never ceased to be said, that lessons in lesson-books are not the whole of education... the highest value of all belongs to the things which children have made entirely themselves... It is of greater value to a child to have grown one perfect flower than to have pulled many to pieces to examine their structure' (Stuart, 1911).

(Her book is free to read online through Gutenberg Press.)

Collecting evidence of learning during open-ended tasks relates to tracking the concepts students uncover and put to work. Their explanations may be more or less scientific to begin with, and you want to allow them to use their unique language. When they see the transformations in the shadows mentioned earlier, they might describe the changes in position in their own way. The shadows *hid* in other shadows. The shadows *grew* longer/shorter, and they *moved* to the right. Children don't need to know the exact angles; just observing the transformations sets them up for great thinking.

Great learning spills into the community

In several schools I have worked with in the past few years, students are making an impact beyond the classroom with their investigations. Children have been so passionate about environmental sustainability that they've written to local councils asking if they can take responsibility for wildlife, use parkland for observations, etc. One six-year-old child asked a restaurateur if he minded if she made and displayed a poster in his café window asking his customers to avoid single-use plastic straws.

An example of this spilling into the community with older children occurred when school-averse boys in Year 10 were allowed to base a project on their interests. They were parkour (urban-running) fanatics. They wrote about their sport and offered to give lessons to younger students in an area of the school where there was soft fill. Their project included physiology, nutrition, biomechanics and statistics. They were keen to have an area where they could train in this incredible sport. On the back of their successful inclusion of a training space and coaching area in their school, they wrote to their local council to ask them to build one for the community. The were invited to give a presentation. Based on their commitment and enthusiasm, the council allocated a seven-figure sum of money to build walls and provide soft fill in a local park!

This is education that is truly alive.

In summary

- Open-ended mobilisation has the educator at three units away and the students have a range of 35° (3:35°)
- Open-ended mobilisation has a curriculum goal, but the learning pathway and assessment tasks are unknown to either the educator or the students at the beginning of the investigation
- The products in this zone can be broad and achieved over a long amount of time or small and done within a single session or day
- Creative products often combine elements from different disciplines, for example, science and music
- The educator is a facilitator who provides materials and scaffolds to help children refine their understanding of concepts
- Evidence can be collected in various ways, including recording conversations and using digital means like video, photography or audio recording. Products can be performed or recorded in portfolios, etc.

Chapter 15
Auto-generative creativity

You can't use up creativity. The more you use, the more you have.
Maya Angelou

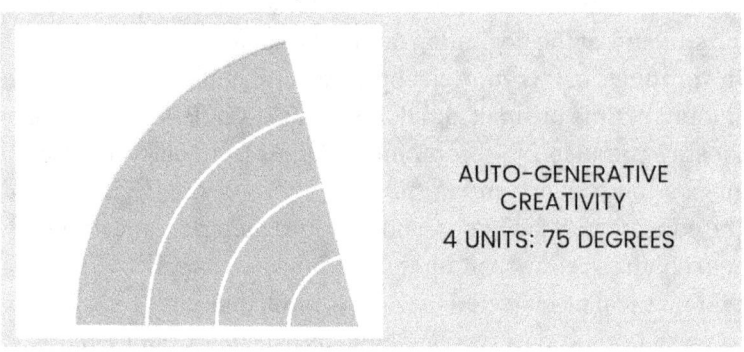

Figure 40: Auto-generative creativity

Coordinates

This zone is at the maximum distance of four units with a range of 75° (4:75°).

Definition

Auto-generative creativity is when a task, goal or activity is started in a person's mind. It might or might not relate to curriculum learning. It could be a unique way of viewing current information and originating a new perspective or significance. It could be a new technique for doing something. It may be the first time a person has discovered and used something known to the world but new to the individual. Once the creative intention, visualisation or action is in the world, it can be shared and used collaboratively. Creativity is mostly born in the mind, but it can also emerge in a state of flow as when a child is immersed in painting or an adult is working with processes and materials. Creativity can occur without external influences or be facilitated as a result of creative prompts.

Educator's role

The educator:

- Harnesses their own interests, passions, learnings and ideas in creative ways in the classroom
- Is overtly respectful of creative ideas and actions students bring to conceptual understanding
- Recognises the auto-generative creativity of students
- Encourages students' self-generative activity and products to launch more advanced learning
- Facilitates and guides the creative process as it is underway
- Lends skills or facilitates by providing access to more materials
- Provides opportunities to imagine and generate creative ideas
- Recognises instances of auto-generative creativity and attunes students to their creative intuition and processes

Students' role

The students:

- Spontaneously access and use a variety of skills, knowledge and processes when approaching a self-projected task
- Develop a product that is unique to them and may be unique to the world
- Are independent and capable of designing tasks but may also discuss with others in collaborative ways to solve problems or develop products

About auto-generative creativity

When children enact their auto-generative creativity, we have made ourselves redundant, and that is when we have done our best job.

In truth, the coordinate dimension of this zone was only added to fit it into the graphic of the agility wheel!

Creativity is infinite, but it is not necessarily automatic. We must develop a mindset to activate creativity. And sometimes, if we follow Edward de Bono's writings, we need to work at it.

In a classroom where children's ideas, products, offerings and wisdom are ignored, devalued or disrupted, they won't learn to use their independent thinking and creative force.

The classroom nuisance

I visited a school and had a 15-minute tea break checking my emails in a small room along a corridor. A seven-year-old lad sidled up to me. He fired a barrage of questions: 'Who are you? Are you coming back into our classroom? What are you doing? Can I play a game on your iPad?'

I answered the questions, then added that he couldn't use my iPad because he was meant to be in his classroom with his teacher and classmates.

'I don't want to go back; anyway, I only come to school to be the classroom nuisance.'

Ummmmm. Flip! I think to myself. How is this for a self-fulfilling Pygmalion moment?

'Really? Don't you like learning?'

'No. I want to stay home and play with my Pokémon.'

'Tell me about Pokémon.'

He tells me how many cards he has and his favourite and least favourite characters. He talks about the video game and the health and damage he must quantify for his characters as they journey through the game. He knows the value of the different trainers and characters. He talks about several characters' skills in attacks and their battle superpowers. He talks about the levels Pokémon evolve through. When Charmander receives enough battle experience, it evolves into Charmeleon and later Charizard. (And there are evolutions beyond that!)

His knowledge of the characters, the statistics and the narratives is complex. His memory about the characters, where they belong in the catalogue and what he still wants to collect, as well as his combined knowledge of video games and card collecting, are highly impressive.

In no way is this a kid who doesn't like learning. He just has not been switched on to learning *in school*.

If he is already outside the learning at seven, how will he get through the rest of his schooling?

Classroom creators

At a school I'd visited earlier in the same week, three six-year-old boys were settled in a small room set off their main classroom constructing a model of the human heart. They were using a heart-shaped chocolate box and thinking about how the heart pumps blood because 'it is a very strong muscle'. It was part of an open-ended investigation into the human body.

In the large classroom, children learn about their hands using three modalities: drawing, writing and digital photography. One child had written, *'I need hands so that I can hold a spoon. Evry (sic) one has lines on their hands. We can feel with our hands and we can eat with our hands.'*

This was May... in Prep! The child then photographed the writing and the realistic drawing with an iPad. He added a few images from a safe search engine to enhance the information. No adult prompted his actions, which included self-correcting an error in his writing!

There were individual representations of the skeletal system on the walls where children had used earbuds, grass straw, matchsticks and many other materials to replicate human bone structure. For most of the lesson, which extended for a couple of hours, not a traditional 45 minutes, the children worked independently or in small groups with access to an endless array of materials. *And not one was labelled a nuisance.*

What inspired you?

Think about your teachers at school. Which of them do you remember with the most fondness and respect? Which experiences over your education influenced your thinking and creativity? Perhaps a gifted teacher even had a hand in who you imagined you might become or which pathway your education would take.

To be creative, you need knowledge. The broader and deeper the knowledge the better. But it would help if you also had encouragement and inspiring models who enact their creativity.

Creativity can occur at any moment and any level within a school day. I have mentioned before the child who made the folded puppets. She is also the child who imagined herself sewing wings and who made a 3D card where a rolled-up column of paper popped up when she opened it. I can still visualise her giggling every time she did it. We might not see it if we are not on the lookout for auto-generative creativity. If we don't value students' independent, creative ideas and products, they might stop offering them.

Creativity occurs in different ways. A child might discover something for themselves before realising that it is 'a thing' in the real world. They notice that when they mistakenly plaster some red paint on the yellow paint, boom bang, orange emerges. Of course, paint mixing is well-known in the world, but this is their personal discovery of it. If they employ it, it is their first creative use of it. Creativity does not have to be completely original or new to the world. It has to be new and original to us.

Within the routines and curricular activity framework, a world of knowing and wondering is revealed. To return to the late Loris Malaguzzi's belief that children have a hundred languages to express themselves, the use of the various means, as described in the classroom above, creates an environment where creation can emerge and flourish.

The underlying reason for this is that all the sensory modalities are engaged, which enhances learning. The hundred languages harness the auditory, visual and kinaesthetic modalities of learning. This idea also resonates with Howard Gardner's theory of multiple intelligences (Gardner, 1993).

To facilitate these languages, emphasis is placed on providing an environment which is rich in possibilities and aims to engage children's interests and experiences. There is an endless variety within the security of a predictable routine. A normality of latent possibility.

The children use these languages not only to demonstrate their knowledge but also to construct knowledge. The same brain function that enables us to remember and organise information from the environment also enables us to create.

A glimpse into the creative brain

The human brain, a most miraculous organ, fascinates me.

Sir Charles Sherrington, Nobel Prize-winner and the grandfather of neurophysiology said that when the brain fires, 'It is as if the Milky Way entered on some cosmic dance' (Sherrington, 1955).

Each human brain has more than one million million brain cells – 1,000,000,000,000. When a thought is triggered, each individual brain cell is capable of contacting and embracing as many as 10,000 or more proximate brain cells. When they communicate, the number of possible combinations in the brain, if written out, would be one followed by 10.5 million kilometres of noughts! (Buzan, 2010)

The brain is the only organ that is mainly formed by interaction with experiences external to it. It is literally created by experience. To be helpful, the experience needs to be positive. When you're labelled a nuisance, the learning happens equally well, just negatively.

The more often the experience is repeated, the more efficient memory and thought become. Each repetition results in myelination, creating an overlay of a white fatty substance that boosts the speed of neural networks. The way to encourage myelination in the brains of our students is to use six principles:

- We learn through all our senses
- We remember well what happened at the beginning (primacy)
- We remember well what happened at the end (recency)
- We remember what we are interested in
- We remember new things we can connect to what is already known
- We remember things that engage our emotions (Buzan & Buzan, 1993)

Each of these principles can be harnessed to support students' creativity.

The genesis of curriculum content and possible projects

I want to shift the conversation from students' creativity to your creativity. You are the most critical resource in your role as an educator. You are the model auto-generator.

My educational practice is a function of my lived experience, and there are so many things I love to do. In my seminars and consultations, I always advise educators to bring their whole selves to the table. If you love patchwork, gardening, astronomy, bottle digging, keeping chickens, model aeroplanes, dirt biking, scrapbooking... anything – bring it!

I have the tremendous fortune to travel a lot.

When I travel, I am always on the lookout. My paternal grandmother, who always planted a fig tree the minute she moved anywhere (useless fact), used to say, 'Lil, you can steal with your eyes.' I've done it all my life. If I see, do, feel or newly understand anything that inspires me, it has the potential to inspire others. So, I consciously curate memories and experiences I can draw on when planning curricula inquiries. Perhaps it's William Blake's illustrations at the Tate Gallery in London; Richard Serra's immense sculptures at the Guggenheim Museum Bilbao; Andy Goldsworthy's phenomenal ephemeral artworks in nature (Goldsworthy, 1989) or an exceptional Alice in Wonderland mixed media exhibition at ACMI in Melbourne in 2019 (ACMI, 2020).

I love Federation Square – so much so that I based a project on it with my colleague, Marg Campbell, in 2005 called 'Line Dance.' Federation Square is the most eclectic collection of lines imaginable: architectural, mathematical and natural. The project crossed multiple disciplines and captured hundreds of ways *lines* are meaningful to children and to society. I think it is still my favourite exploration ever.

In 2019 I had the exceptional joy and honour of convening a public exhibition of Reggio Emilia-inspired contributions from ten schools entitled: 'Reimagining Children, Spaces and Relationships.' It was held in the Atrium at Federation Square, the piazza of Melbourne.

Within my role at Independent Schools Victoria (ISV), my colleague Helen Schiele and Dr Stefania Giamminuti had been working with the schools for three to four years before the exhibition. It was an early years component of ISV's second biannual Arts Learning Festival, 2–4 May 2019. This ground-breaking ISV event crosses education sectors and international boundaries and celebrates *unlimited imagination*. It honours the importance of arts in education and provides events for schools, students, families and the community. The exhibition was achieved in partnership with the Reggio Emilia Australian Information Exchange (REAIE) and included bringing to Australia two remarkable speakers, Paola Strozzi and Filippo Ciele, from the Reggio Children organisation. The value of this endeavour was in the number of people brought together in a significant creative collaboration.

To commence curricular planning, with everything I love and everything that interests me in the background, I use Tony Buzan's six prompts mentioned earlier and his mind-mapping process, and put down everything I know about the idea I want to explore. I gather everything my friends and colleagues know. I read up, go online, look for visuals and watch videos. I go out and take photographs, visit the places I might want to take children and contact the experts I want to invite.

Then the real planning begins. I usually map out my ideas for the different ways a project can be explored across the arts, the sciences and particularly movement and performance arts. Once all that is set out, I search for a beginning.

The first encounter with ideas and materials will ignite children's interest. (The primacy effect.) It was not unusual for me to spend half the night setting up an installation just for the beginning of a project and then taking it down the next night because, as you all well know, the space is needed by someone else the day after! But it was always worth it. One of the extremely important things about a project is documenting the encounter. The photographs, video, conversations and children's responses are fuel for later on when the learning is unpacked more deeply.

Whether it is medieval, outer space, light and shadow or things that roll, there should be a good beginning. And the beginnings don't all have to be productions. The early introductions of the Explorations project were just well-placed, hands-on experiences that were in the room for two to three weeks before we even discussed them. We just observed what the children did with ice, the water play area, pipettes, coloured water, etc. They were prefiguring the later, deeper and more complex work to come.

The end of projects is also important. They might be the performance on the day you have family visitors or a special celebration like Harmony Day, or Footy Day. At one school where I worked in 2000, the year of the Sydney Olympics, we had a mini Olympics. Each year level explored a sport or some aspect of the iconic Olympic movement. My group was immersed in the long jump – and they loved it. We had our own team emblem, flag, mascots and class long jump records – it was a blast.

You could have a book launch or show a film at a red carpet event.

Between a good start and a good end, the senses, interests and adding to prior knowledge happen – even the enhancement of children's conceptual knowledge!

The brain can transport us to other places, other times and other possibilities.

We can create what never existed before.

The school is not only a place for transmitting culture, but for creating it. We can create a culture that supports creativity. We should all try to create and maintain a culture of respect for children and their innate ability to construct their learning with us. They will interpret and change the try as they become the builders of the future.

It is our task to guide towards many metamorphoses. In Reggio Emilia, there is a saying: 'Nothing without joy!' I have always found this mantra energising and inspiring.

In summary

- Auto-generative creativity is when students or educators use prior and newly acquired knowledge to solve a problem in a unique way or design a product that is unique to them or the world
- A culture of respecting creativity will allow it to flourish
- When students have understood and can independently mobilise, deploy and use the knowledge they have gained, we are made redundant – our job is done

Chapter 16
The agile educator

Intelligence is the handmaiden of flexibility and change.
Vernor Vinge – *A Fire Upon the Deep*

Throughout this book, I have spoken about knowing things well first and then using the knowledge in unique and flexible ways across different contexts later. This is transfer.

Having outlined seven distinctive learning zones, I now ask you not to regard them as standalone and unrelated. Of course, you can plan to use a zone consciously and implement it on its own. But, at any moment, in any zone, you can engage what you know about another zone. This is often referred to as incidental teaching. You know about incidental teaching; I'm sure you've used it. However, with clear knowledge of each zone, the repertoire for your educational action and intervention increases in range.

In the middle of free play, a child shows you a leaf. Some people say, 'That's nice, honey'. You recognise the learning opportunity. Do you engage the zone of mediated play, or even clarity of concept for the duration of your conversation? Do you note the interaction because, in the curriculum, you are planning a life sciences investigation? Do you suggest the child collects a few more leaves to put on the light table for wax crayon rubbings on translucent paper? Do you notice that the leaves around you provide a perfect matching, sorting and counting activity? Which way will you turn? Where do you pivot? When you know the zones well, you can instantly recognise and harness opportunities for each kind of learning.

Pivoting between giving children range and narrowing the focus is calibrating between independent, mediated and scripted learning.

Children need all of these to move upwards through zones of proximal development. They need to be challenged continuously, but at the appropriate level and in a way that keeps their minds active.

The agile educator is at the centre of the agility wheel. Educators can consciously deploy a learning zone and also be ready to pivot in an instant if it is immediately beneficial for an individual or group of children. This is the creative use of your knowledge, competence and skills.

Conversation about creativity

Creativity has always been a departure point of this book. The idea is not to be limited by a two-part model. Edward de Bono says surprisingly that 'the brain is not designed to be creative'. He suggests that creativity can be engendered by 'deliberate and systematic techniques that can be used in a formal manner' (De Bono, 1993).

We have to wake our brains up and move them out of patterns of thinking, routines, habitual behaviour and even the appreciation of the known, tried and tested.

I once interviewed the principal of a prestigious private school to present a project on developing students' metacognition and personalising learning. The principal listened, then responded that the ideas were highly appealing, but the school was running too well, the parents were too happy and the students were achieving enviable results. There was no reason to fix what was working well.

Don't fix what's not broken

There is absolutely nothing wrong with that.

But I would like to put a spanner in the work just for your consideration.

To do that, I am offering you four prompts for creative thinking:

- A bird's-eye view
- The maze
- The branch
- The ladder of aspiration

These prompts are completely open-ended, and you can apply them in any way or in any context.

A bird's-eye view

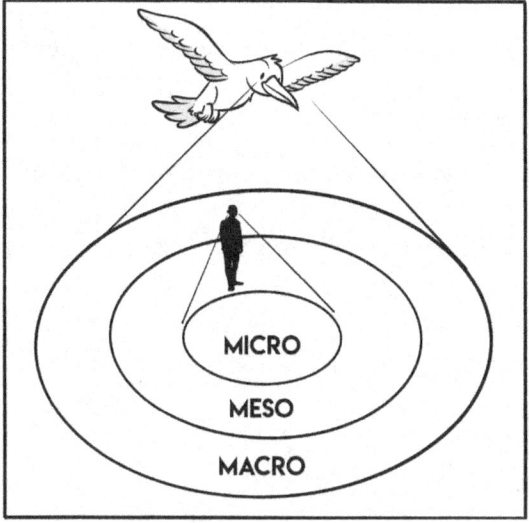

Figure 41: Bird's-eye view

In relation to the bird's-eye view prompt, let's return to the principal who loved the idea of innovation, but was very comfortable with the school's performance, and unwilling to make any changes.

When something is running really well, it can be because you've been doing it for ages, and it works. You have your 46 boxes packed and are ready to break one open every week. Or, it can be because you have periodically put your head up, surveyed the landscape and *continue to evaluate* it as the best way to run your process. You still believe your students' outcomes and achievements are current and valuable.

What you do every day can be characterised as a micro landscape. It is set within a broader landscape, the macro environment. There are many influential forces at work in the macro environment. They have the power to impact the micro word in the immediate term, in the medium term and in the long term. An example of an immediate influence was the disruption of COVID-19 on global education. Because of its urgency, it could not be ignored. Other forces are not as visible, and an effort needs to be made to identify what might be shaping things from beyond the microspace.

The bird's-eye view prompt encourages you to expand your perspective occasionally to assess what is happening in your microenvironment in relation to current and emerging macro forces.

We will look at this at the corporate, educator and student levels.

Corporate viewpoint

The forces from the macro environment are regularly summarised by the term PESTLE, thought to have originated by Harvard professor Francis Aguilar in the 1960s. The model refers to the constellation of forces below:

- Political
- Economic
- Social
- Technological
- Legal
- Environmental

Some organisations assessing shaping forces adapt this model and include additional areas that are important to them. One inclusion I think is necessary is 'ethical', so you might consider it STEEPLE. I also like to extend 'social' to 'sociocultural' because it implies a recognition of inclusive practice.

Any place of education needs to be aware of what is happening in the macro space.

The bird's-eye view has three concentric circles: micro, meso and macro as seen in Figure 41 on page 169. A figure in the centre has a circumscribed vision. A bird hovers with a much broader perspective. The prompt asks us to broaden our perspective to refine our decision-making, our current practice and particularly our future practice.

If you notice something on the horizon, that means you will have to transform some elements of your micro world, you can start to work on it. For it not to be too disruptive, the creativity prompt provides a meso space: a place in between your streamlined micro efficiency and the direct impact of the macro world.

Your meso space becomes a space for research and pre-planning. If you are a leader, you might like to offer reading materials or professional learning opportunities to key staff members. You might create an innovative teacher research project within the routine practice to assess the impact of the new ideas. If the outcomes of the research are positive, the meso space is where you plan the means to disrupt the microenvironment and bring your community on board with the new thinking.

I have seen this in operation at a school with multiple-year levels. Leaders in the early years arena implemented changes via mini research projects. When parents were startled by changes they saw in the classroom, they complained. The school leadership asked for things to return to the old 'normal'.

But the innovative early years' educators stood their ground and asked for the grace of time. For a few months, they tracked maths and literacy competency using the same assessment tools they had in the past. They compared the new normal results against old normal results, and were able to present evidence of improvement.

Over time, the research in the early years saw transformations in practice from the infant rooms, through primary and middle school to secondary students. The conceptualisation of the role of the educator, the image of students and the image of leadership changed dramatically.

The parents were brought on board. It is now a principle that early communication with parents, and even parent involvement in decision-making in some endeavours, has changed the relationship between the school and the community.

So, work in the meso space can have an enormous impact on the micro space. It can be done with considered intention. Evidence can be collected and tracked. It is possible to address the forces from the macro environment in a manageable, staged way.

The educator viewpoint

This broadening of perspective does not only occur at the institutional level. You can apply it to your personal practice or, if you are lucky enough to work within a collaborative professional learning team, to a small group of colleagues.

The idea is to give yourself permission to explore, research and implement transformations in a manageable, fluid and trackable way. You might like to investigate new techniques, so you learn about them and plan how to implement and include them in what you are already doing. You have a play in the meso space. This might be reading, listening to others or visiting. The visit can be as simple as going into colleagues' teaching spaces, or it might be to another school, state or country!

The student viewpoint

When you assess students, you make assumptions and come to conclusions about your immediate observations. But you can implement the bird's-eye view in relation to the student, too.

The PESTLE model for students might be:

- **P**erformance
- **E**motion
- **S**ocial
- **T**echnical
- **L**anguage
- **E**xperiment

Rather than relying on surface observations, expand your perspective to consider more than what meets the eye.

A student's performance (P) relates to the entire way the child is integrated into the learning space. It is the combination of how they perform on tasks, their ability to deal with routine and change, their interactions with others and their general attitude to learning.

If you want to check in to see how any of these elements might be enhanced, you can ask yourself questions about what might be affecting the child's emotional energy (E) or social competence (S). Technical (T) refers to where they are in their skill levels for a task, whether it is how to cut with scissors or structure a problem-solving task.

Assess their facility with language (L). Have they consolidated a concept? Are they ready for more complex language? Are they battling because the main language is not their home language? Do they need coaching on how to express their feelings or information? Don't forget to tune in to body language and tone when they communicate because that is often where you will see what is really happening. All of these questions will give you ideas about how you can structure change for the child.

The experiment (E) part involves creating a mini research project in which you propose introducing a strategy. An example from my practice was that a child who had elements of Asperger's syndrome had difficulty staying on task during the day. I carried out a 10-minute planning session with him before the doors opened each day. We discussed and drew the tasks and then the plan was put in his locker. We could refer back to the plan whenever he lost his way or motivation. I also left periods of the day free for him to follow his own path. The partnership in pre-planning, the interleaving of planned and unplanned time and the consistency all had powerfully positive results in his performance.

It is essential to apply this thinking to every student. Sometimes, our focus is so riveted on children battling in some way that we forget to enhance their performance and prepare them for a rise in their zone of proximal development.

The maze

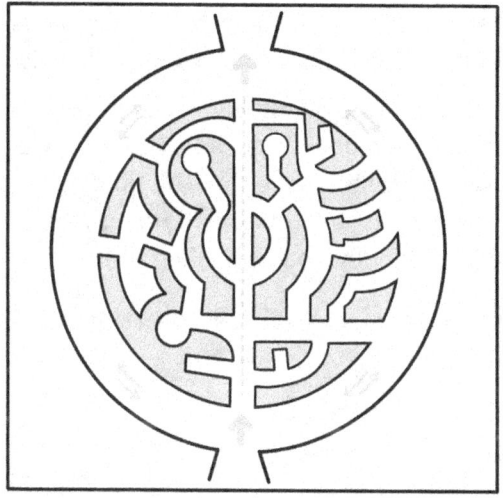

Figure 42: The maze

PESTLE invites you to look outward to see what impacts your profession and practice.

The maze is an internal landscape. It invites you to pause and reflect inwardly on where you are and where you might want to be. A direct route through the maze represents a clear and simple path from here to there. If you are totally comfortable you're on the right track, you can ignore everything else about the maze. In our lives, we have times like this when we are in flow and the road seems clear.

But if your vision is unclear, you might like to pause for a moment in the maze. Is there something you want to do to clarify your goals? Do you want to spend more time deepening your knowledge about yourself, your practice and your environment before you move forward? Is there something else you want to be doing in your life? Does where you are suit your values, your sense of self and your aspirations? If parts of the maze don't serve you and are fruitless dead ends, close them off.

Not all dead ends are bad dead ends. There are some termini where you might like to spend some time and enjoy the scenery. These cul de sacs might not lead you through the maze but are valuable in themselves.

And there are different ways out of the maze towards your goals than the direct route.

Robert Frost ponders over 'The Road Not Taken'. If you take a chance and head down a different path, you will learn to navigate its challenges and intricacies. The diversion can add to your expertise, knowledge and wisdom.

The maze is an invitation to genuinely check in to your internal space and see if you want to trek directly ahead or take a diversion, even if you don't exactly know where it will take you. This kind of deep reflection may prompt you to stay where you are, or you might realise you want to be somewhere else. Consider the road not taken.

The branch

Figure 43: The branch

The branch is a prompt about seeing a connection.

Say you pick up a leaf and it is labelled with the word 'grit'. How do you interpret it?

You pick up another leaf and it reads 'soccer ball'.

A third leaf is labelled 'compression'.

Take a moment and try to make some connections.

You will definitely be able to because our brain is constantly trying to make sense of things so it can know them and turn them into comfortable, predictable pieces of information. Unless we make connections, information exists as a standalone piece. It is not part of the bigger picture. We want children to see how things connect. We want them to have a big picture or concept and the details.

The words I offered – grit, soccer ball and compression – will make more sense if I explain their origins.

The branch prompt has a main branch that is a content focus. It divides into two boughs to represent the adoption of two different disciplines to explore the content. I wanted to use a completely abstract idea as the starting point for content, so in the middle of a walk with a friend, I came up with the word 'bounce'.

Where would it take you if you had the word as a content prompt? Write down one or two ideas before I relate my ideas. 'Bounce' suggested two areas of exploration for me. The first was the laws of physics and the second was the concept of resilience.

If we go down the physics route, the work with children can be really fun and exciting. They can be offered several different kinds of objects to explore their bouncing properties. They can talk about how different efforts when you bounce a particular ball can change the height of the bounce. The direction in which you bounce the ball can change where it bounces to. Children will explore an object's ability to return to its original shape after being stretched or squeezed. An example I researched online used a rubber ball, a ping pong ball and a marble.

You can provide any number of materials, and children can imagine what makes things bounce. Whether they actually get to the point of using the language of elasticity is not really that important. The process of observing, planning, predicting and theorising is good enough.

If they understand the properties of bouncing back after a bump, it takes us to the other discipline of psychology: mindset. Grit is the ability to bounce back and be resilient – to return to form after something has stretched or bounced you out of shape!

Understanding grit, soccer ball and compression together, rather than as isolated ideas, gives the investigation clarity. We want to spend time on the leaves and have multiple leaves; but we want to know that the information is connected at a deeper, clearer level.

I would love to know what other abstract ideas you generate as prompts for learning.

The ladder of aspiration

Figure 44: The ladder of aspiration

I think the ladder image is very clear. What do you want to achieve? What are the four steps you can immediately take to get there? This is not to say that the steps can be instantly achieved, but as you rise up one step, you will know what the next part of the process is. I know you will continue aspiring to new goals in your practice. Your role as an educator is vitally important and I wish you great success as you climb your ladders of aspiration.

Appendix
Lists for educators

No weapons are more potent than brevity and simplicity.
Katherine Cecil Thurston

The absolute basis of this book is to scaffold children's conceptual understanding from an early age, engaging their minds and imagination at a level appropriate to their current zone of proximal development and paving the way for future learning.

This part of the book is a collection of lists that I hope will act as references to help you achieve the goal outlined above. As we know, Brendan Bartlett sees the list as a helpful language structure. I hope you find them useful.

Appendix contents

- 13 universal relationships
- 20 key concepts for organising knowledge and drawing out meaning
- A dozen thinking skills
- 5 senses
- Weather words
- 10 modalities for learning
- Play ideas and equipment
- Social, emotional and cultural concepts and skills

13 universal relationships

It is through some kind of relationship that everything in the universe connects. The relationships largely answer the grand old question starters: Who, What, Where, When, How and Why?

13 universal relationships for all levels of learning

Qualifying	What/who is it?
Analytical	How can it be analysed into whole and parts?
Functional	How does it work? What makes it work? And why?
Temporal	When is it placed in sequence and time?
Spatial	Where is it located or related in space?
Comparative	How is it similar, equivalent or different? And why?
Causal	What is the cause and effect? And why?
Dependent	What depends on what? And why?
Transformational	How and what has changed and why?
Quantifying	How is it estimated or measured for precision and accuracy?
Hypothetical	If something happens, what might follow? And why?
Imaginative	Wondering what, where, when, how and why something might be.
Ethical	What is whose responsibility to something?

20 key concepts for organising knowledge and drawing out meaning

colour	dimension	distance	emotion
form	function	length	location
material	orientation	pattern	perspective
senses	shape	size	speed
temperature	time	volume	weight

Superordinate concept	Elements that belong to the concept
colour	primary, pastel, shade, hue, light, dark, tone, red, blue, yellow, green, purple, orange, violet, indigo, black, white
dimension	length, width, height, area, volume, weight, density, speed, volume (sound), distance, pressure, angles, temperature, wavelength, interval, unit
distance	metric, kilometres, imperial, miles, light years
emotion	happy, sad, angry, excited, surprised, fearful, disgusted (Each of these has multiple associated labels. It is important for students to distinguish both the broad and subtle differences in emotions.)
form	Forms that are not Euclidean shapes are included here: bulbous, thorny, tentacled, etc. Each example needs to be examined and described. There are some wonderful natural forms: symmetrical, radiant, divergent, convergent, pinnate, linear, spiral, concentric, webbed, tessellated, fractal
function	Functions are individual to entities, so need to be assessed in situ. Look at the internal workings and external impact of any object, entity or system. Examples are: transport, measurement, locomotion, recording sound, mixing food, etc.
length	metric, millimetre, centimetre, metre, kilometre, imperial, inch, foot, yard, mile
location	above, around, at, back, before, behind, below, beside, centre, down, far, front, in, inner, left, middle, near, next to, north, on top, on, out, outer, right, south, underneath, up, within
material	concrete, cork, glass, leather, metal, natural materials, paper, Perspex, plastic, polystyrene, porcelain, rubber, shell, sponge, stone, wood
orientation	Generally, orientation refers to the universal directions and coordinates we use to locate ourselves in space: north, south, east, west (all the in-between measures), longitude, latitude
pattern	Any identifiable recurring trend. Patterns can be labelled, e.g. ABAB, ABBA, AABBCC, etc. Patterns can be seen in materials but also in all the phenomena around us, like moon cycles, seasons, etc. We can see patterns of behaviour and many other kinds. These patterns also relate to the forms above.

Superordinate concept (cont.)	Elements that belong to the concept
perspective	Similar to orientation, perspective is the position you view things from. This can be a physical perspective but also attitudinal, psychological, social, political and other perspectives. Students benefit from learning about perspective in a variety of ways.
senses	Sight, hearing, smell, taste and touch all have concepts related to them. We can also refer to our inward senses and intuitions. See the senses table on page 182.
shape	**One-dimensional linear shape:** crenellated, curved, parallel, round, straight, wavy **Two-dimensional shapes (geometric):** diamond, dodecagon, hexagon, octagon, parallel, parallelogram, pentagon, polygon, quadrilateral, rhombus, square, triangle **Curved Shapes:** arc, circle, ellipse, oval, parabola **Three-dimensional shapes:** cone, cube, cylinder, polyhedrons; 3D shapes with straight sides: prism, pyramid, sphere, torus (like a donut)
size	diminutive, microscopic, minuscule, minute, small, medium, middling, midsized, regular, colossal, enormous, huge, large, massive
speed	cadence, dashing, fast, hastening, hurried, hurtling, moderate, motoring, rate, rhythm, sedate, slow, slow-moving, steady, whizzing, zooming
temperature	ambient, baking, blistering boiling, Celsius, chilly, cold, degrees, Fahrenheit, freezing, frosty, heat, icy, tepid, thermal, thermometer, warm
time	12 hours, 24 hours, afternoon, age, always, am, annual, biannual, century, contemporaneous, contemporary, continual, continuous, dawn, day, decade, dusk, early, aeon, era, evening, future, half-hour, hour, late, midday, millennium, millisecond, minute, moment, month, morning, never, new, night, now, old, past, permanent, pm, present, quarter-hour, second, soon, temporary, then, today, tomorrow, week, year, yesterday, young
volume	litre, millilitre, pint, quart
weight	heavy, light, gram, milligram, kilogram, ounce, pound, stone

A dozen thinking skills

1. **Focus and attention.** No learning can take place without focus and attention. It implies self-regulation. Attention may be directed to a single object or a complex task. Irrelevant stimuli are ignored. When there is a complex field, the focus needs to be directed in a systematic way to gather all relevant information. (Often left to right or top to bottom.)
2. **Labelling.** Language is the essential toolkit for thinking and learning. Precise meaning should be attached to each label. Labels denote phenomena in both the concrete and abstract domains. They can be contextual. Labels apply to simple and compound ideas. (Like electro-magnetism.) All parts of the compound idea need to be understood. Labels may be understood in receptive language before they are readily communicated in expressive language.
3. **Spatial perception.** Understanding position and orientation. Each thing is positioned or oriented in relation to something else. Spatial perception involves different points of view. Some spatial information is informed from a personal perspective depending on which way the viewer faces, like left, right, front or back, and other information relates to universal reference points like north, south, vertical and horizontal.
4. **Temporal perception.** Understanding time, sequence and order.
5. **Representation.** Human beings have developed innumerable ways of representing reality and ideas. These may be verbal, pictorial, graphic, symbolic, etc. Representation can be simple, like the word 'blue' representing the colour blue, or highly complex, like mathematical symbols, for a combination of abstract ideas. Students' performance will become limited to the point where they lose track of what representations and symbols mean.
6. **Comparison.** Understanding how things are equivalent, similar or different. Comparison is achieved by focusing on specific criteria in both a focus entity A and a target entity B. It can be simple when one object is compared with another object, but it becomes highly complex when one system of interrelated elements is compared to another. For example, comparing the circulatory system of reptiles versus mammals. Comparison is the basis for categorisation because it reveals how things belong or do not belong in a group. When comparing, equivalence, similarity and difference can be noted. It is important to remember that, depending on the focus feature, a single entity can belong to more than one category. A red circle can belong to a colour category and a shape category. This is the basis of Venn diagrams. At a higher level of thinking, comparison is the basis for decision-making and evaluation. A further key aspect of comparison is to keep track of what remains the same and what has changed or transformed. For example, if six oranges have been cut into quarters, there are 24 pieces, but the fact remains that all the parts originate from six oranges. This is the conservation of constancy – tracking what is the same.

7. **Visualisation.** Mentally represent things in the mind. This may be a single visualisation or a complex manipulation of information. Visualisation can relate to the present, past and future.
8. **Identifying relationships.** Internal relationships exist between a whole and its parts. People can move, because they have feet and legs. External relationships exist between a whole and another whole. A torch, a lamp, a tail light and a chandelier are related because they all project light. Some relationships are determined with reference to a specific criterion internally or externally. One box is bigger, has greater volume and is sturdier than another. Relationships might be contextual. Nurses, hospitals, ambulances and emergency care are related. Some relationships are causal: x happened because of y. I checked my Facebook and burnt the toast... again.
9. **Problem-solving.** Perceive a problem, assess it and develop a plan to solve it. Gather full and complete information, discard irrelevant information, combine more than one source of information, plan the sequence of steps, enact the steps and solve the problem.
10. **Providing logical evidence.** Using what is known, often from several sources, explains occurrences. It is related to inferential thinking, whereby conclusions are drawn based on evidence.
11. **Hypothetical thinking.** Hypothetical thinking is 'if-then' thinking. It uses available information to project what might happen, or to visualise alternatives. It is related to the scientific method but can be used in all areas of life.
12. **Imagination.** Imagination can occur at many levels. It can be a simple image or lead to endless possibilities. It is the fuel of creativity. Sir Ken Robinson considered the two in this way: 'Imagination allows us to think of things that aren't real or around us at any given time, creativity allows us to do something meaningful with our imaginations' (Robinson & Aronica, 2010).

5 senses

sight	blind, blurry, clear, dark, glance, glimpse, keen, light, observe, outlook, panorama, peripheral vision, range of vision, scenery, see, sight, spy, stare, survey, unclear, visibility, vista, witness
sound	alliteration, animal sounds, bang and crash sounds, distant, drone, echo, insect sounds, knock, loud, high, low, mechanical sounds, movement sounds, musical pitch, natural sounds, onomatopoeia, rattles, sibilance, sirens and signals, soft, volume, weather sounds

taste	acidic, bitter, chewy, creamy, crisp, crumbly, crunchy, dense, dry, al dente, fluffy, fresh, gelatinous, granular, gritty, herby, hot, light, liquid, lumpy, oily, powdery, runny, saccharine, salty, savoury, smooth, soggy, solid, sour, spicy, stale, stodgy, sweet, tart
smell	aromatic, cloying, damp, fetid, floral, foul, fragrant, fresh, fumes, herby, malodorous, musty, perfumed, pleasant, pungent, smoky, spicy, sweet
touch	ache, agony, bruised, bumpy, cold, constricted, corrugated, crackly, cramp, crisp, dry, firm, fluffy, furry, fuzzy, gritty, grooved, hard, hot, icy, itchy, loose, lumpy, massage, moist, mushy, numb, oily, painful, pat, pinch, pins and needles, plump, prickly, pummel, ridged, rough, rubbery, satiny, scaly, scratchy, silky, slap, slippery, smack, smooth, soft, sore, spongy, stroke, swollen, tickly, tight, velvety, warm, waxy, woolly, wrinkly

Weather words

breezy, bright, cloud, cold, cool, fog, hail, humid, mild, mist, overcast, rain, sleet, snow, storm, sunny, thunder and lightning, warm, windy

10 modalities for learning

1. **Concrete:** using or manipulating objects in the real world.
2. **Verbal:** related to the use of language for accessing, assessing, processing or expressing learning. There are two main aspects to the verbal modality: oral and written.
3. **Symbolic:** related to any symbols recognised or developed to represent something else. Examples are road signs, letters, numbers and the table of elements. Students can create their symbols to share information or understand the symbols in their daily lives and curriculum.
4. **Pictorial:** relates to images representative of reality, such as life-like drawings or photographic materials. Pictorial is differentiated from graphic (see number 6 below) because pictures are less abstract and more accessible than graphic formats. Graphic formats may have some symbolic elements that have to be learned.
5. **Figural:** relates to anything to do with form or shape.
6. **Graphic:** relates to drawings that may or may not include easily recognisable representations of information. Examples are line drawings and graphic organisers. The drawings are more abstract than pictures and may include some elements of what it is representing. Or it relates to a representative way

to express complex information in an easily absorbed format, for example, graphs, diagrams and models.
7. **Digital:** refers to any use of digital devices and may include many other modalities. Digital technology enables students to combine many modalities quickly and easily, and it requires a particular kind of technological skill and know-how.
8. **Kinaesthetic:** refers to capturing information in movement. This can be single movements and sensations captured through the senses or a complex sequence of movements. Movement and sensation are harnessed as a vehicle for complex communication. (Embodied cognition.)
9. **Representational/metaphorical:** refers to the ability to develop an idea or concept representing some aspect of an object, relationship or abstract concept. It usually makes it easier for the learner to understand something else's complexity through something known or understood.
10. **Imaginary:** relates to the ability of the mind to explore new ideas or knowledge. This can be a fairly simple or an extremely complex mental construct for learning and problem-solving.

Play ideas and equipment

Home corner	Imaginary play themes	Outdoor play
Furniture:	castle	A-frames
bed	cultural	balancing beams
bookcase	cultural celebrations	baskets
chairs	fairy tale	brooms
cot	fire station	buckets
cupboard	home/kitchen	climbing rocks
divider	medical	cooking utensils
sink	office	digger trucks
stove	police	fabric
table	school	fixed climbing, swinging,
Props:	shop	flying fox, etc
bedclothes	superheroes	large building blocks
dolls	transport	musical chimes
dress-up items	hair salon	platforms
empty grocery containers		PVC piping
play money		rakes
pots and pans		sandpit
scale		scrapers
tea set		see-saw
wooden people		spades
		watering cans
		woodwork equipment

Sports and activities	Recycled and decorative materials	Construction and tabletop toys
balls beanbags big blocks cycles hockey hoola hoops lengths of rope natural materials parachute quoits skipping ropes skittles soccer walking stilts	bottles cardboard boxes cardboard cylinders dowel sticks jars lengths of fabric lengths of timber natural materials plastic containers rubber timber offcuts various manufacturing offcuts wishing stones	blocks Duplo games gears LASY Lego matching and sorting Meccano puzzles sequencing stickle bricks tessellation What's in the Square?

Social, emotional and cultural concepts and skills

Self- and home-care skills	• Dressing • Bedtime • Bath time • Mealtime • Pet care • Travel and commuting • Play • Cooking and baking • Setting the table • Building and construction • Setting up and packing away
Gross- and fine-motor skills	• Pick up food and objects • Use cutlery • Use crockery • Lift body • Roll • Sit • Crawl • Bounce • Balance • Walk • Run • Hop • Skip

Gross- and fine-motor skills (cont.)	• Jump • Roll • Slide • Climb • Swing • Hang • Alternate movements fluidly • Pinch • Clasp • Lift • Cut • Paste • Carry objects • Arrange materials • Hold and use painting, drawing and writing implements • Roll (e.g. plasticine and clay) • Stack objects • Balance objects
Social and cultural concepts	• Identity • Self • Other • People • Humanity • Relationship • Emotion • Friendship • Family • Culture • Society • Religion • Love • Respect • Inclusion
Social interactions	• Greet others • Make eye contact (if culturally appropriate) • Engage in conversation • Take turns • See things from another's point of view • Help others • Accept help from others • Be cooperative • Be collaborative • Be aware of what is happening in the environment

Social interactions (cont.)	• Take care of another • Self-regulate behaviour • Self-regulate emotions • Move beyond the need for instant gratification • Engage in rites of passage • Share in cultural events • Understand roles and rituals in different cultures, religions and ethnic groups	
Emotional intelligence (EQ)	• Understand emotions • Name emotions • Understand others' emotions • Name others' emotions • Develop self-talk strategies to withstand negative emotions • Develop a routine/strategy for dealing with conflict • Be empathetic • Be sympathetic • Understand boundaries • Respect boundaries • Understand the consequences of behaviours • Deal with the consequences of behaviours • Learn to separate the person from the behaviour • Understand that no emotional state is permanent • Predict emotional impact • Accept that emotions are part of life	
Curriculum areas to explore	**Arts and crafts** • Understand materials and how they may be used • Mark making • Organise marks and/or ideas on page, canvas • Interpret images and artworks • Design and execute 2D and 3D products • Explain the work • Understand space and spatial relationships • Understand time and temporal relationships • Interpret and investigate gesture and body language • Learn about motion, posture and the interpretative dance • Drama • Puppetry	
	Science and nature • Observe and record information • Develop and test hypotheses • Carry out experiments • Melting, freezing and evaporation of water	

Curriculum areas to explore (cont.)	• Food processes during baking and cooking • Electricity • Magnetism • Life cycles of animals and plants • Physical properties of matter: e.g. glue dries hard, clay dries to become unmalleable • Energy and combustion • Properties of air • Biological processes: breathing, nutrition, digestion • Growth and development • Modes of communication: digital, wireless, internet • The senses: processes of sight, hearing, touch, taste, smell • The brain: thinking, imagining, creating, connecting, learning, etc.
	Mathematics • Number knowledge • Counting • Estimate • Measure • Collect and sort materials • Make groups and sets • Build patterns • Geometric shapes and attendant knowledge • Add and subtract • Divide and multiply • Graph • Understand terminology • Understand symbols • Understand grouping symbols for equations • Explain relationships • Represent the ideas in numerical, spatial, concrete and other ways • Apply/transfer mathematical procedures as listed above
	Verbal literacy This includes oral speech and written language: • Listen to sounds • Identify sounds • Talk in single words • Combine words • Use sentences • Identify words and match them with real-world equivalents • Identify words with what is known but is not immediately present

Curriculum areas to explore (cont.)	• Identify words with what is neither known nor immediately present using imagination • Listen to stories • Monitor the sequence and plot • Understand stories • Tell stories • Remember and relate experiences • Understand similarities and differences • Identify causal relationships • Predict events and routines • Visualise • Follow conversations • Recognise that a book uses language of image and word • Know that images and words have meaning • Identify words • Read words and sounds • Identify images • Understand images
	• Read sounds • Read words • Read sentences • Read full texts • Read stories • Identify characters • Identify relationships between characters • Follow the plot • Follow the argument of structure of a text • Distinguish what is more and less important • Understand the chronological aspects of the narrative • Understand analogies • Understand what is implicit in the text • Understand different formats of text • Understand how the text is organised

Bibliography

ACMI. (2020). *Making Wonderland documentary*. Retrieved from https://www.youtube.com/watch?v=rnIquw8qYg0&abchannel=ACMI%28Australian CentrefortheMovingImage%29

Anderson, L., Kratwohl, D., Airasian, P., K.A., C., Mayer, R., Pintrich, P., & Wittrock, M. (Eds) (2001). *A taxonomy for learning, teaching and assessing*. New York: Longman.

Atherton, F., & Nutbrown, C. (2013). *Understanding schemas and young children – Birth to three*. London: SAGE.

Baratta-Lorton, M. (1994). *Mathematics their way: An activity-centered mathematics program for early childhood education*. Pearson.

Bartlett, B. (2003, Volume 1). Valuing the situation: A referential outcome for top-level structures. *Reimagining practice: Researching change*, pp. 16-37.

Ben-Hur, M. (2006). *Concept-rich mathematics instruction*. USA: Association for Supervision and Curriculum Development (ASCD).

Biggs, J. (2016). *Academic, SOLO taxonomy*. Retrieved 9 March 2016, from John Biggs, writer, traveller and academic: http://www.johnbiggs.com.au/

Bodrova, E., & Leong, D. J. (1996). *Tools of the mind – The Vygotskian approach to early childhood education*. New Jersey, United States: Prentice-Hall Inc.

Bruner, J. (1973). Going beyond the information given. In J. Ed Anglin, *Beyond the information given* (pp. 218–238). New York: Norton.

Buzan, T. (2010). *Use your head – How to unleash the power of your mind*. Harlow, UK: Pearson Education.

Buzan, T., & Buzan, B. (1993). *The mind map book*. London: Butler and Tanner.

Cagliari, P., Castagnetti, M., Giudici, C., Rinaldi, C., Vecchi, V., & Moss, P. (2016). *Loris Malaguzzi and the schools of Reggio Emilia: A selection of his writings and speeches, 1945-1993*. New York: Routledge.

Castagnetti, M., & Vecchi, V. (Eds) (1997). *Shoe and meter (Scapra e metro)*. Reggio Emilia: Reggio Children.

Costa, A. (2008). *Learning and leading with habits of mind*. USA: ASCD.

Covey, S. (2013). *The 7 habits of highly effective people*. USA: Rosetta Books LLC.

Darling-Hammond, L., Barron, B., Pearson, D. P., Schoenfeld, A. H., Stage, E. K., Zimmerman, T. D., & Chen, M. (2008). *Powerful learning – What we understand about teaching for understanding*. San Francisco: Jossey-Bass.

De Bono, E. (1993). *Serious creativity – Using the power of lateral thinking to create new ideas*. Glasgow: Harper Collins.

De Bono, E. (1998). *Lateral thinking & the use of lateral thinking*. Penguin Books, Australia.

Doenmez, S. (2020). *The threshold concept framework can lead to transformative learning*. Retrieved from https://www.nais.org/magazine/independent-school/summer-2018/threshold-concept-framework/

Donaldson, M. (1984). *Children's Minds.* London: Fontana.

Dweck, C. (2006). *Mindset: The new psychology of success.* New York: Random House.

Eather, J. (2020). *A maths dictionary for kids.* Retrieved from http://www.amathsdictionaryforkids.com/

Edwards, C., Gandini, L., & Foreman, E. G. (Eds) (1998). *The hundred languages of children: The Reggio Emilia approach advanced perspectives.* Greenwich: Ablex Publishing Corporation.

Ellis, K., Denton, D., & Bond, J. (2013). An analysis of research on metacognitive teaching strategies. *Procedia social and behavioural sciences*, 4015-4024.

Epstein, D. (2019). *Range.* PAN.

Falikman, M. V. (2014). Cognition and its master: new challenges for cognitive science. In C. University, A. Yasnitsky, R. Van der Veer, & M. Ferrari (Eds.), *The Cambridge handbook of cultrual-historical psychology.* UK: Cambridge University Press.

Feuerstein Institute. (2020). *International centre for enhanced learning potential (ICELP).* Retrieved from https://www.icelp.info/

Feuerstein, R., Feuerstein, R., & Falik, L. (2009). *The Feuerstein instrumental enrichment basic program.* Jerusalem: The Feuerstein Institute.

Feuerstein, R., Rand, Y., Hoffman, M., & Miller, R. (1980). *Instrumental enrichment: An intervention program for cognitive modifiability.* USA: Scott, Foresman & Co.

Gardner, H. (1993). *Frames of mind – The theory of multiple intelligences.* London: Fontana Press.

Gardner, H. (2000). *The disciplined mind.* Hammondsworth, UK: Penguin.

Gentner, D. (2005). The development of relational category knowledge. In L. Geschkoff, & D. H. Rakison, *Building object categories in developmental time* (pp. 245-275). New Jersey: Erlbaum.

Goldsworthy, A. (1989). *A collaboration with nature.* Green Apple Books.

Goleman, D. (1995). *Emotional intelligence.* New York: Bantam.

Guskey, T. R. (2001). *Benjamin S. Bloom's contributions to curriculum, instruction and school learning.* University of Kentucky.

Hansen, A. (2014). *BCS curriculum in kindergarten and school 2009.* Retrieved from https://researchgate.net/publication/258316586

Haywood, H. C. (Ed.). (2003). Contemporary Issues in Psychological and Educational Assessment: A Special Issue of peabody Journal of Education (1st ed.). Routledge. https://doi.org/10.4324/9781410608161

Hill, R. (2016). *Kant's schematism and time determinations.* Retrieved from https://exordiumuq.org/2016/07/19/kants-schematism-and-time-determinations-by-rosie-hill/

Horvath, J. C. (2019). *Stop talking and start influencing.* Chatswood: Exisle Publishing.

IBO. (2020). *Primary years program.* Retrieved from International Baccalaureate Organisation: https://www.ibo.org/programmes/primary-years-programme/

Jenny, E. (2020). *A maths dictionary for kids.* Retrieved from http://www.amathsdictionaryforkids.com/

Kilpatrick, J., Swafford, J., & Bradford, E. (2001). *Adding it up: Helping children learn mathematics.* Washington, D.C.: National Academy Press.

Kinard, J. T., & Kozulin, A. (2008). *Rigorous mathematical thinking.* Cambridge University Press.

MacRae, C., & Jones, L. (2019). *A philosophical reflection of the 'Leuven Scale' and young children's expression and involvement.* Retrieved from https://www.tandfonline.com/doi/full/10.1080/09518398.2020.1828650

McLeod, S. (2019). *What is the zone of proximal development?* Retrieved from https://www.simplypsychology.org/Zone-of-Proximal-Development.html

Meadows, S. (1993). *The child as thinker – The development and acquisition of cognition in childhood* (First edition ed.). Guildford, UK: Routledge.

Montessori, M. (1965). *Dr Montessori's notebook.* New York: Schocken Books.
Piaget, J., & Cook, M. T. (1952). *The origins of intelligence in children.* New York: International University Press.
Project Zero; Reggio Children. (2001). *Making learning visible – Children as individual and group learners.* (C. Giudici, & M. Krechevsky, Eds.) Reggio Emilia: Reggio Children.
Reggio Children. (1990). *Everything has a shadow except ants.* Reggio Emilia: Reggio Children.
Rieber, R. W., Carton, A. S., & (eds). (1987). Thinking and speech. In R. W. Rieber, & A. S. Carton (Eds.), *The collected works of L.S. Vygotsky. vol 1: Problems of general psychology.* New York: Plenum Press Development.
Rinaldi, C. (2001). The pedagogy of listening. *Innovations in early education: The international reggio exchange,* Vol 8, no. 4.
Ritchhart, R. (2002). *Intellectual character.* San Francisco: Jossey-Bass.
Robinson, K., & Aronica, L. (2010). *The element: Finding your passion changes everything.* Penguin.
Ronilo, A. (2018). Effectiveness of metacognitive instruction on students' science learning achievement: A meta-analysis. *SSRN.*
Schonkoff, J. P., Phillips, D. A., & (Eds). (2000). *From neurons to neighbourhoods – The science of early childhood development.* Washington, D.C.: The National Academy of Sciences.
Sherrington, C. S. (1955). *Man on his nature.* Harmondsworth: Penguin Books.
Singer, D. G., Golinkoff, R. M., & Hirsh-Pasek, K. (2006). *Play=Learning: How play motivates and enhances children's cognitive and social-emotional growth.* New York: Oxford University Press.
Skemp, R. R. (1986). *The psychology of learning mathematics.* England: Plenum.
Stuart, J. E. (1911). *The education of Catholic girls.* The Gutenberg Project.
Suskind, D. (2015). *Thirty million words – Building a child's brain.* New York: Dutton.
Vygotsky, L. (1978). *Mind in Society: The development of higher psychological processes.* Cambridge: Harvard University Press.
Vygotsky, L. (1986). *Thought and language (A. Kozulin translation and ed.).* Cambridge: MIT Press.
Wabisabi. (2020). *How to ask the right inquiry-based questions.* Retrieved from https://wabisabilearning.com/blogs/inquiry-asking-inquiry-based-learning-questions
Walker, K., & Bass, S. (2015). *Early childhood play matters.* ACER Press.
Watanabe-Crockett, L. (2018). *Future-focused learning.* USA: Solution Tree.
WEHImovies. (2020). *Organelles of a human cell.* Retrieved from https://www.youtube.com/watch?v=2YCgro6BV8U&ab_channel=WEHImovies
Whitely, G. (Director). (2015). *Most likely to succeed* [Motion Picture].
Wikipedia. (2020). *Holography.* Retrieved https://en.wikipedia.org/wiki/Holography
Yasnitsky, A., Van Der Veer, R., Ferrari, M., & (Eds). (2014). *The Cambridge handbook of cultural-historical psychology.* Cambridge: Cambridge University Press.
Zhu, P. (2016). *Digital agility: The rocky road from doing agile to being agile.* Bookbaby.

Dedication

This book is dedicated to:

Pierre, my exceptional husband, whose love, support, insights and patience are the wind beneath my wings.

To my talented children, Sean and Candice, and your partners, Judy and Eric. Your enthusiastic interest in all my endeavours – no matter how wild – inspires me.

To my late parents, Bob and Bee, whose care and unwavering encouragement instilled a deep love of education in me.

To my siblings, Helene and Martin, whose accomplishments stand as a testament to our shared foundation.

To my friends and network, whose steadfast support and camaraderie have been a constant source of strength. Thank you for being part of this incredible journey.

And to everyone who has shared in this journey, thank you for giving me a sense of belonging.

About the author

Lili-Ann's journey began in the vibrant city of Johannesburg, South Africa, where she lived with her parents, Bob and Bee, and her siblings, Helene and Martin. With her father's work in the gold mines, the family frequently relocated, turning each new place into an adventure. From a young age, Lili-Ann cherished moments with her grandparents and discovered a love for ballet and piano lessons. Inspired by her favourite author, Enid Blyton, she entertained her siblings with imaginative, made-up stories.

While she was at university, Lili-Ann met Pierre, the love of her life. Together, they built a joyful and fulfilling life in South Africa with their two children, Sean and Candice. Lili-Ann's career took off as she specialised in early childhood education, finding immense satisfaction in shaping young minds.

In 1998, a significant chapter began when Lili-Ann and her family moved to Australia. Embracing their new home, they forged strong friendships and immersed themselves in various activities, all while keeping cherished ties with lifelong friends from their youth. Their adventures took them across Europe and America, with skiing emerging as a beloved family holiday tradition.

More recently, Lili-Ann has added 'author' to her list of accomplishments. She has published this book, *The Power of Play*, a book for educators, *Roots and Wings*, a guide for parents and *Lifelong Vitality – Twelve Pathways to Ageing Youthfully*, a book for those ageing gracefully. Her early life experiences, vivid imagination and deep-seated passion for education continue to inspire her creative and professional endeavours.

www.ingramcontent.com/pod-product-compliance
Lightning Source LLC
Chambersburg PA
CBHW050357120526
44590CB00015B/1727